All Is But Fantasy

A musical adaptation.

Whitney White

methuen | drama

LONDON • NEW YORK • OXFORD • NEW DELHI • SYDNEY

METHUEN DRAMA

Bloomsbury Publishing Plc, 50 Bedford Square, London, WC1B 3DP, UK
Bloomsbury Publishing Inc, 1359 Broadway, New York, NY 10018, USA
Bloomsbury Publishing Ireland, 29 Earlsfort Terrace, Dublin 2, D02 AY28, Ireland

BLOOMSBURY, METHUEN DRAMA and the Methuen
Drama logo are trademarks of Bloomsbury Publishing Plc

First published in Great Britain 2026

Copyright © Whitney White, 2026

Whitney White has asserted her right under the Copyright, Designs
and Patents Act, 1988, to be identified as author of this work.

Cover design by Mecca McDonald

All rights reserved. No part of this publication may be: i) reproduced or transmitted in
any form, electronic or mechanical, including photocopying, recording or by means of
any information storage or retrieval system without prior permission in writing from
the publishers; or ii) used or reproduced in any way for the training, development or
operation of artificial intelligence (AI) technologies, including generative AI technologies.
The rights holders expressly reserve this publication from the text and data mining
exception as per Article 4(3) of the Digital Single Market Directive (EU) 2019/790.

Bloomsbury Publishing Plc does not have any control over, or responsibility for, any
third-party websites referred to or in this book. All internet addresses given in this
book were correct at the time of going to press. The author and publisher regret any
inconvenience caused if addresses have changed or sites have ceased to exist, but
can accept no responsibility for any such changes.

No rights in incidental music or songs contained in the work are hereby granted and
performance rights for any performance/presentation whatsoever must be obtained
from the respective copyright owners.

All rights whatsoever in this play are strictly reserved and application for performance
etc. should be made before rehearsals to Creative Artists Agency, 405 Lexington
Avenue, 19th Floor, New York, NY 10174, Attn: Kevin Lin & Ally Shuster.
No performance may be given unless a licence has been obtained.

A catalogue record for this book is available from the British Library.

Library of Congress Control Number: 2026933034.

ISBN: PB: 978-1-3506-3928-7
       ePDF: 978-1-3506-3930-0
       eBook: 978-1-3506-3929-4

Series: Modern Plays

Typeset by Westchester Publishing Services
Printed and bound in Great Britain

For product safety related questions contact productsafety@bloomsbury.com.

To find out more about our authors and books visit
www.bloomsbury.com and sign up for our newsletters.

ABOUT THE ROYAL SHAKESPEARE COMPANY

The Royal Shakespeare Company (RSC) is a leading global theatre company that sparks local, national and international conversations that build connections, create opportunities and bring joy.

We passionately believe that great storytelling can change the world, and that theatre offers its own unique form of storytelling: it's live and shared, and transforms a group of strangers into audiences who, together, experience a story come to life in front of their eyes.

We collaborate with the most exciting artists to tell the stories of our time, and through a range of programmes we nurture the talent of the future.

We perform on three stages in our home in Stratford-upon-Avon, in London and in communities and schools across the country and around the world.

Our transformative Creative Learning and Engagement programmes reach over half a million young people each year.

Support us and make a difference; for more information visit **www.rsc.org.uk/support**

@thersc
Registered Charity no. 212481

All Is But Fantasy was first performed at The Other Place Studio Theatre in Stratford-upon-Avon on 22 January, produced by the Royal Shakespeare Company. The cast was as follows:

WOMAN	**WHITNEY WHITE**
MAN	**DANIEL KRIKLER**
FIRST WITCH	**RENÉE LAMB**
SECOND WITCH	**GEORGINA ONUORAH**
THIRD WITCH	**TIMMIKA RAMSAY**
DESDEMONA/SHADOW JULIET	**JULIETTE CROSBIE**

MUSICIANS

PIANO	**TOM KNOWLES**
GUITAR	**NICK LEE**
BASS	**CHEVELLE FRAZER-ROSE**
DRUMS	**FÉZ OGUNS**

Prior to the Royal Shakespeare Company premiere as *All Is But Fantasy, Emilia, Juliet,* and *Richard III* were commissioned by the American Repertory Theater at Harvard University [Diane Paulus, Artistic Director, Diane Borger, Executive Producer] and *Lady Macbeth* had its world premiere under the title *Macbeth in Stride*, produced by the American Repertory Theater, and subsequently produced by Shakespeare Theatre Company Washington, DC, Philadelphia Theatre Company Philadelphia, PA and Brooklyn Academy of Music Brooklyn, NY.

The RSC Acting Companies are generously supported by The Gatsby Charitable Foundation

New Work at the RSC is generously supported by Hawthornden Foundation and The Drue and H.J. Heinz II Charitable Trust

CREATIVE TEAM

WRITER, DIRECTOR & COMPOSER	**WHITNEY WHITE**
SET & COSTUME DESIGNER	**SOUTRA GILMOUR**
LIGHTING DESIGNER	**RYAN DAY**
SOUND DESIGNER	**TONY GAYLE**
CHOREOGRAPHER	**SARITA PIOTROWSKI**
MUSIC SUPERVISOR	**SIMONA BUDD**
MUSIC DIRECTOR	**TOM KNOWLES**
FIGHT DIRECTOR	**KATE WATERS**
INTIMACY DIRECTOR	**LUCY HIND**
DRAMATURG	**RÉJANE COLLARD-WALKER**
CASTING DIRECTORS	**CHARLOTTE SUTTON** CDG **CHRISTOPHER WORRALL** CDG
VOICE COACH	**NIA LYNN**
ASSOCIATE CHOREOGRAPHER	**CHRISTOPHER TENDAI**
ASSISTANT DIRECTOR	**MUMBA DODWELL**
ASSISTANT MUSIC DIRECTOR	**FALK MEIER**
PRODUCTION MANAGER	**LUCY GUYVER**
COSTUME SUPERVISOR	**CHRIS CAHILL**
PROPS SUPERVISOR	**ALISON TANQUERAY**
COMPANY MANAGERS	**SUZANNE BOURKE** **PIP HOROBIN**
COMPANY STAGE MANAGER	**PIPPA MEYER**
DEPUTY STAGE MANAGER	**ROSE BURSTON**
ASSISTANT STAGE MANAGER	**HANNAH GILLETT**
ASSISTANT PRODUCER	**ELLA SUTTON**
PRODUCER	**JOE ROSE**

This text may differ slightly from the play as performed.

CAST

JULIETTE CROSBIE
DESDEMONA/SHADOW JULIET

RSC DEBUT SEASON: *All Is But Fantasy.*

THEATRE INCLUDES: *A Christmas Carol* (The Old Vic); *Circle of Friends* (Breda Cashe Productions/Gaiety Theatre); *Where Sat the Lovers* (Malaprop Theatre Co); *Last Orders at the Dockside* (Abbey Theatre); *Me, Sara* (Abbey Theatre/national tour/Peacock Theatre); *Measure for Measure* (Fortune's Fool).
MUSICALS IN CONCERT INCLUDE: Royal Philharmonic Orchestra: *Christmas Cracker 2025.* The Hallé, Manchester: *Movies and Musicals*. BBC National Orchestra of Wales: *Friday Night Is Music Night*. RTE Concert Orchestra: *Movies and Musicals* (Bord Gáis Energy Theatre); *Disney 100, A Celebration of Andrew Lloyd Webber, New Year's Eve Gala* (NCH).
TELEVISION INCLUDES: *How to Get to Heaven From Belfast* (Hat Trick Productions); *Borderline* (ShinAwil); *Harry Wild* (Acorn TV).
FILM INCLUDES: *Everybody Digs Bill Evans* (Hot Property Films/Screen Ireland/BFI); *Power Ballad* (Treasure Entertainment); *Baite* (Cine4); *Royal Rendezvous* (E! Entertainment); *Don't Go Where I Can't Find You* (Samson Films); *The Other Lamb* (Rumble Films).

DANIEL KRIKLER
MAN

RSC: *All Is But Fantasy, Wendy & Peter Pan* **(Barbican, London).**

TRAINED: Central School of Speech and Drama, Laine Theatre Arts.
THEATRE INCLUDES: *Fiddler on the Roof* (Regent's Park Open Air Theatre/Barbican, London); *Austenland* (Savoy Theatre); *Natasha, Pierre and the Great Comet* (Donmar Warehouse); *The Motive and the Cue, The Normal Heart* (National Theatre); *The Book Thief* (Leicester Curve); *The Secret Life of Bees* (Almeida); *The Tempest, A Midsummer Night's Dream, Macbeth* (Guildford Shakespeare Company); *Fighting Irish* (Belgrade); *Pippin* (Charing Cross Theatre); *4000 Miles, Present Laughter* (The Old Vic); *Unicorns, Almost* (Bristol Old Vic); *Homos, Or Everyone in America* (Finborough); *Pink Mist* (Bristol Old Vic/UK tour); *Jersey Boys* (Dodger Productions); *Mamma Mia!* (Novello); *Bare: A Pop Opera* (Union Theatre); *Loserville* (Garrick/West Yorkshire Playhouse). Whilst training: *A Serious Case of the Fuckits, The Heresy of Love.*
FILM AND TELEVISION: *The Halcyon* (Leftbank Pictures for ITV).

RENÉE LAMB
FIRST WITCH

RSC DEBUT SEASON: *All Is But Fantasy.*
TRAINED: Tring Park School for the Performing Arts.
THEATRE INCLUDES: *Radiant Boy* (Southwark Playhouse); *Passing Strange* (Young Vic); *Little Shop of Horrors* (Regent's Park Open Air Theatre); *Fantastically Great Women Who Changed the World* (UK tour); *Six the Musical* (Arts Theatre); *Be More Chill* (The Other Palace/West End); *Malory Towers* (Wise Children); *Ain't Misbehavin'* (Mercury Colchester/Southwark Playhouse); *Cake* (Lyric Theatre/The Other Palace).
TELEVISION INCLUDES: *Sweetpea* (Sky); *This Town* (BBC One).
FILM INCLUDES: *The Running Man, This is the Night Mail.*

GEORGINA ONUORAH
SECOND WITCH

RSC DEBUT SEASON: *All Is But Fantasy.*
TRAINED: ArtsEd, where she was awarded the Andrew Lloyd Webber Foundation Scholarship, and Emil Dale Academy.
THEATRE INCLUDES: *Brigadoon, Shucked* (Regent's Park Open Air Theatre); *Hamilton* (Victoria Palace); *Little Shop of Horrors* (Sheffield Crucible); *Kiss Me, Kate* (Barbican, London); *Oklahoma!* (Wyndham's Theatre); *Dick Whittington* (National Theatre); *Bad Cinderella* (Gillian Lynne Theatre); *Millennials* (The Other Palace); *The Wizard of Oz* (London Palladium). Workshops include: *Midnight* (Harlequin Theatricals); *The Children's Inquiry* (National Theatre Studio); *The Enormous Crocodile* (Roald Dahl Story Company); *Mandela* (Young Vic).

TIMMIKA RAMSAY
THIRD WITCH

RSC DEBUT SEASON: *All Is But Fantasy.*
TRAINED: Rose Bruford College.
THEATRE INCLUDES: *Guys & Dolls* (Bridge Theatre); *Moulin Rouge* (West End); performance at the London Stage Debut Awards (2024); *Madagascar the Musical* (UK and Ireland tour); *Cinderella* (Lyric).
TELEVISION INCLUDES: *Horrible Science, Horrible Histories, Ghosts, Enterprise* (BBC); *The Other One* (Tiger Aspect/BBC1); *The Larkins* (ITV); *Adult Material* (Channel 4).

WHITNEY WHITE
WRITER/DIRECTOR/COMPOSER
WOMAN

RSC DEBUT SEASON: *All Is But Fantasy.*
Whitney White is an Obie and Lilly Award-winning and Tony Award-nominated director, actor and musician, who showcases her bold and innovative approach of storytelling through her many productions, both on and off-Broadway.

THEATRE INCLUDES: *Macbeth in Stride* (Brooklyn Academy of Music, for which she also wrote book, music and lyrics). As Director: (Broadway): *Liberation, The Last Five Years, Jaja's African Hair Braiding.* London: *The Secret Life of Bees* (Almeida). NYC Off-Broadway: *Saturday Church, Walden, Jordan's, Soft, On Sugarland, The Spectacularly Lamentable Trial of Miz Martha Washington, A Human Being of a Sort, An Iliad, The Amen Corner, Othello, Canyon, Jump, What to Send Up When It Goes Down, Our Dear Druglord, For All the Women Who Thought They Were Mad.*

FILM AND TELEVISION INCLUDES: *Ocean's Eight, Single Drunk Female, Louie, The Playboy Club.* Whitney also wrote for season one of Boots Riley's *I'm a Virgo* (Prime Video).

OTHER: Whitney received a special honour at the 2025 Drama League Awards with the Founders' Award for Excellence in Directing and is a Rolex Arts Protège. MFA Brown University, BA Northwestern.

CREATIVE TEAM

SOUTRA GILMOUR
SET & COSTUME DESIGNER

RSC: *All Is But Fantasy, The Winter's Tale, Ben and Imo* (RSC/Orange Tree), *Timon of Athens* (RSC/TFANA Brooklyn).

THEATRE INCLUDES: *Waiting For Godot, A Doll's House* (Broadway); *Woman In Mind, Evita, Much Ado About Nothing, The Tempest, Just For One Day, The Commitments, From Here To Eternity, The Lover, The Collection* (West End); *Sunset Boulevard, Betrayal* (Broadway/West End); *Two Strangers (Carry a Cake Across New York)* (ART/West End/Broadway); *The Effect, Twelfth Night, Les Blancs* (National Theatre); *Merrily We Roll Along* (New York Theatre Workshop); *The Secret Life of Bees, Macbeth, Reasons to be Pretty* (Almeida); *Further Than the Furthest Thing, Bull* (Young Vic); *The Seagull* (Playhouse Theatre); *Cyrano de Bergerac* (BAM/NY/West End); *Running With Lions, Out West* (Lyric Hammersmith); *Romeo and Juliet* (Lyttelton Films for the NT); *& Juliet* (Shaftesbury Theatre/Broadway); *Pinter at the Pinter* (Harold Pinter Theatre); *Guys & Dolls* (Royal Exchange); *Knives in Hens, Inadmissible Evidence, Piaf* (Donmar); *Apologia, Richard III, The Maids, The Homecoming, Macbeth* (Trafalgar Transformed/Jamie Lloyd Company); *The Guards at the Taj* (Bush Theatre); *My Brilliant Friend* (NT/Rose, Kingston); *Pitchfork Disney, Killer* (Shoreditch Town Hall); *I See You, The Pride* (Royal Court); *Assassins, Merrily We Roll Along* (Menier Chocolate Factory); *Reasons to be Happy* (Hampstead); *Urinetown* (St James, West End); *The Crucible, The Duchess of Malfi* (The Old Vic); *The Caretaker* (Sheffield Crucible/Tricycle).

OPERA INCLUDES: *Breaking the Waves* (Scottish Opera); *Jack the Ripper* (ENO); *Evita, The Turn of the Screw* (Regent's Park Open Air Theatre); *Quartett, Iris* (ROH); *Iris* (Opera Holland Park); *Carmen, Saul, Hansel and Gretel, Anna Bolena, Don Giovanni, Cosi Fan Tutte* (Opera North); *Mary Stuart, The Birds, Trouble in Tahiti* (English Touring Opera).

Soutra Gilmour has received six Olivier Award nominations and two Tony Award nominations including Best Set Design for *Betrayal* and Best Costume Design for *Cyrano de Bergerac*, and a London Standard nomination for Best Set Design for *Much Ado About Nothing*.

RYAN DAY
LIGHTING DESIGNER

RSC: *All is But Fantasy, Macbeth, The Constant Wife, The Red Shoes, Pericles* (RSC/Chicago Shakespeare Theater).

TRAINED: The Royal Central School of Speech and Drama.

THEATRE INCLUDES: *Hamlet, Never Have I Ever* (Chichester Minerva); *The Beautiful Future is Coming* (Bristol Old Vic); *Pimpinone* (Linbury, Royal Opera House); *The Da Vinci Code* (Salisbury Playhouse/Mercury Theatre); *In the Mouth of the Wolf* (Barn Theatre); *Handbagged* (Queen's, Hornchurch); *Twelfth Night* (National Youth Theatre); *A Marvellous Party* (Prince of Wales); *The King's Speech* (Watermill); *The History Boys* (Theatre Royal Bath/UK tour); *Now, I See* (Stratford East. 2025

Offie Award for Best Lighting Design); *The Lion Inside* (Rose Theatre/international tour); *The Boy at the Back of the Class* (Rose Theatre/UK tour); *Backstairs Billy* (Duke of York's); *Quiz* (Chichester Festival Theatre/UK tour); *Saving Face* (Curve Leicester/The Place); *Black Superhero* (Royal Court); *Local Hero* (Co-Lighting Designer with Paule Constable. Chichester Minerva). As Associate/Assistant: *The Rite of Spring* (Sadler's Wells/UK tour); *Wickies* (Park 200); *The Lemon Table* (Salisbury Playhouse/UK tour); *Les Misérables, Les Misérables in Concert* (Sondheim).
OTHER: Ryan won Best Lighting Design (*Body of Work*) at the Black British Theatre Awards 2024.

TONY GAYLE
SOUND DESIGNER

RSC: *All Is But Fantasy, My Neighbour Totoro* (West End/Barbican, London 22-23 and 23-24).
THEATRE INCLUDES: For Sound Design: *Wild Rose* (Royal Lyceum); *The Lonely Londoners, The Purists* (Kiln); *Becoming Nancy* (Birmingham Rep); *Play On!* (Talawa Theatre Co); *Shifters* (West End/Bush Theatre); *Next to Normal* (West End/Donmar Warehouse); *Fan Girls, School Girls; Or, The African Mean Girls* (Lyric Hammersmith); *Two Strangers (Carry a Cake Across New York)* (West End/Kiln); *Gatsby* (American Repertory Theater); *High Times and Dirty Monsters* (Liverpool Playhouse); *Sizwe Banzi is Dead* (Mayflower); *Pygmalion, Sylvia, The 47th* (The Old Vic); *Beneatha's Place* (Young Vic); *Greatest Days, Beautiful: The Carole King Musical, Salad Days, American Idiot* (UK tour); *Disney's Aida* (Holland); *Newsies* (Troubadour Wembley Park Theatre); *Kinky Boots* (New Wolsey); *Playboy of the West Indies* (Birmingham Rep); *Legally Blonde* (Regent's Park Open Air Theatre); *Running with Lions* (Talawa/Lyric Hammersmith); *Spring Awakening, And Breathe...* (Almeida); *Get Up, Stand Up! The Bob Marley Musical* (Lyric Theatre); *The Wiz* (Hope Mill Theatre); *A Place for We* (Talawa/Park); *Bue/Orange* (Theatre Royal Bath); *Gin Craze* (Royal & Derngate); *The Living Newspaper, Shoe Lady* (Royal Court); *Poet in da Corner* (Royal Court/UK tour); *Songs for Nobodies* (Wilton's Music Hall/West End); *Floyd Collins* (Wilton's Music Hall); *The Wild Party* (The Other Palace) and *Lazarus* (King's Cross Theatre).
AWARDS: Best Sound at the 23rd Annual WhatsOnStage Awards for *My Neighbour Totoro* (RSC), Black British Theatre Awards (BBTA) Light and Sound Recognition Award 2019 and 2021.
OTHER: Wise Children Trustee, Stage Sight Co-Director.

SARITA PIOTROWSKI
CHOREOGRAPHER

RSC: *All Is But Fantasy, Cyrano de Bergerac, The Tempest.*
Sarita Piotrowski is a choreographer and movement director working across theatre, opera, TV and film.
CHOREOGRAPHY INCLUDES: *Carrie the Musical* (RCSSD); *Three Little Pigs* (Unicorn/Chichester Festival Theatre); *Larmes de Couteau, Full Moon in March* (Royal Opera House); *Been So Long* (Netflix), *Reflection Route* (British Museum);

Sher Yadet Nare (Manoto TV); *Glimpses* (The Place Theatre); *Anything Goes* (Hackney Empire); *Louder than Words* (feature film).
THEATRE INCLUDES: As Movement Director: *The Talented Mr Ripley* (TH Productions/UK tour); *Stars* (Tamasha/Brixton House); *Three Hens in a Boat* (Watermill Theatre); *A Raisin in the Sun* (Lyric Hammersmith/UK tour); *A Taste of Honey* (Royal Exchange); *Hansel and Gretel* (Shakespeare's Globe); *A Playlist for a Revolution* (Bush Theatre); *Dixon and Daughters* (National Theatre); *The Rape of Lucretia* (Britten Pears Arts/Royal Opera House); *Favour* (Bush Theatre); *Jitney* (The Old Vic); *The Glass Menagerie* (The Duke of York's Theatre); *Offside* (Futures Theatre); *Theodora* (Royal Opera House/Teatro Real Madrid); *Jitney* (Headlong/Leeds Playhouse); *The Cunning Little Vixen* (Opera Holland Park); *A Day in the Death of Joe Egg* (Trafalgar Theatre); *I Would Rather Go Blind* (Omnibus Theatre); *Underwater Love* (Futures Theatre); *Nell Gwynn* (Ivy Theatre); *Awa's Journey* (Arcola). As Associate Movement Director: *Tartuffe* (Birmingham Rep); *Best of Enemies* (Young Vic); *Nine Night* (National Theatre). As Intimacy Coordinator: *Branwen: Dadeni* (Wales Millennium Centre).

SIMONA BUDD
MUSIC SUPERVISOR

RSC: *All Is But Fantasy*.
WORK INCLUDES: As Musical Director: *Mean Girls* (Savoy Theatre); *Dreamgirls* (original UK tour); *Heathers the Musical* (original UK production at The Other Palace/Theatre Royal, Haymarket); *Maiden Voyage* (Southwark Playhouse). She has recorded the award-winning *Heathers* Original London Cast Album. Simona is currently Associate Music Supervisor for the UK tour of *Mean Girls*. Media work includes soloist for *Mercedes* and *National Lottery* radio advertising campaigns, conductor at the world premiere of Disney's *A Christmas Carol* and Musical Director for the *British Media Awards*, *Financial Risk Awards* and *Your Money Awards*. She has been a Performance Coach for the ITV productions of *Newsrooms' Got Talent*.
OTHER: Simona works as a guest lecturer, advisor and consultant on musical theatre workshops and courses. Many of these engagements are undertaken for leading specialist performing arts and drama colleges of higher and further education. For a number of years, she was involved with the cabaret circuit across London which included a residency at The Pheasantry – one of London's most recognised cabaret venues.

TOM KNOWLES
MUSIC DIRECTOR

RSC: *All Is But Fantasy*, and as Associate Musical Director on *Hamlet Hail to the Thief* (RSC/Factory International).
Tom Knowles is a composer, music director, orchestrator and pianist. Tom has worked on *MJ: The Musical* as Associate Musical Director (West End): as Musical Supervisor for *Wuthering Heights* at the National Theatre and UK tour (Off-Broadway and US tour transfer) as well as cover conductor on *Heathers* (The Other Palace). Other credits include: *Rebecca* (Charing Cross Theatre) and *Follies* (Tangier, directed

by Rob Ashford). Composition credits include: *GPEC* (28 Dance Exercises 2021); *Signifying Nothing* (SATB/Royal Albert Hall/Birmingham Symphony Hall). Dep credits include Keys 1 for *Bat Out Of Hell, Matilda The Musical* and *South Pacific* (UK tours); *Spirited Away* (Coliseum); *Sinatra The Musical* (Birmingham Rep); *Guys & Dolls* (Bridge Theatre); *Kiss Me Kate, Anything Goes* (Barbican, London); *Groundhog Day* (The Old Vic); *Tammy Faye* (Almeida); Keys 2 for *The Producers* (Garrick); *Newsies* (Troubadour); *Wicked* (UK tour); *The Third Man* (Menier Chocolate Factory).

KATE WATERS
FIGHT DIRECTOR

RSC: *Henry V, All Is But Fantasy, The Boy Who Harnessed the Wind, Hamnet.*
THEATRE INCLUDES: *Evita, Much Ado About Nothing, The Tempest* (Jamie Lloyd Company); *Sunset Boulevard, Cyrano de Bergerac, The Ruling Class, Macbeth, Richard III* (ATG/Jamie Lloyd Company); *High Noon, Othello, Stereophonic, The Great Gatsby, Barcelona, The Hills of California, The Maids, The Pride, The Hothouse, East is East* (West End); *Tina – the Tina Turner Musical* (West End/tour); *Bacchae, Hamlet, Alterations, The Grapes of Wrath, The Father and the Assassin, The Effect, Small Island, Much Ado About Nothing, Frankenstein, One Man Two Guvnors, War Horse, Othello, Women Beware Women* (National Theatre); *The Curious Incident of the Dog in the Night-Time* (National Theatre/West End); *Richard II, Guys & Dolls, A Midsummer Night's Dream, Julius Caesar* (Bridge Theatre); *Animal Farm* (Theatre Royal Stratford East); *Arcadia, The Brightening Air* (The Old Vic); *Macbeth* (Wessex Grove); *King Lear, Portia Coughlan, The Secret Life of Bees, The Tragedy of Macbeth* (Almeida).
TELEVISION INCLUDES: *Coronation Street, Emmerdale* (ITV); *Hollyoaks* (Lime Pictures/Channel 4); *EastEnders* (BBC), all as a regular fight director.
FILM INCLUDES: *My Policeman* (Amazon Studios); *Death of England* (Sky Arts); *Romeo and Juliet* (Sky Arts/PBS).
MUSIC VIDEO: *Always Some MF* by Matt Maltese (Bad Bones Films).
OTHER: Kate has been an Equity Registered Fight Director since 2001. She is also a qualified boxing coach and is a development coach on the England Boxing Performance Pathway.

LUCY HIND
INTIMACY DIRECTOR

RSC: ***All Is But Fantasy, Wendy & Peter Pan* (Choreography/Barbican, London), *Miss Littlewood* (Movement).**
CREDITS INCLUDES: As Movement Director: *Inter Alia, Ugly Lies the Bone* (National Theatre); *The Brightening Air* (The Old Vic); *A Man For All Seasons* (Theatre Royal Bath); *Waiting for Godot* (Theatre Royal Haymarket); *Minority Report, Best Exotic Marigold Hotel, Calendar Girls* (UK tour); *Girl from the North Country* (The Old Vic/West End/Broadway/Australian and US tours); *Murder on the Orient Express* (Chichester Festival Theatre); *Hamlet* (Young Vic); *The Light in the Piazza* (Southbank Centre/Los Angeles Music Center/Lyric Opera of Chicago); *Local Hero* (Royal Lyceum, Edinburgh); *The Last Ship* (Princess of Wales, Toronto/US tour); *Sleeping*

Beauty (Theatr Clwyd); *The Divide* (The Old Vic); *No's Knife* (The Old Vic/Abbey, Dublin); *The Effect, Playing for Time, Twelfth Night, This Is My Family* (Sheffield Theatres); *Multitudes, The House That Will Not Stand* (Tricycle). As Choreography Director: *Spend Spend Spend* (Royal Exchange); *101 Dalmatians* (UK tour); *Oliver!* (West Yorkshire Playhouse); *Awesome Animals and Mini Me* (Three Arrows Media for Sky TV); *Billy Elliot* (Curve Leicester); *The Last Ship* (Northern Stage); *Hansel and Gretel, Thumbelina, The Snow Queen, The Nutcracker, Peter Pan* (BBC); *Truth Seekers* (Amazon Studios); *The Merchant of Venice* (Shakespeare's Globe/US tour). As Intimacy Director: *A Knight's Tale* (Manchester Opera House); *The Fear of 13* (Donmar Warehouse); *Hope Has a Happy Meal* (Royal Court); *Secret Life of Bees* (Almeida); *Groundhog Day* (The Old Vic); *Kerry Jackson* (National Theatre).

RÉJANE COLLARD-WALKER
DRAMATURG

RSC: *All Is But Fantasy, Julius Caesar, Falkland Sound, The Box of Delights, The Magician's Elephant, Tartuffe.*
Réjane is a Dramaturg, and the RSC's New Works Contracts Manager. As part of her role for the company, she is responsible for all contractual negotiations for writers, rights holders, dramaturgs and literary creatives. She is also attached to selected RSC commissions and classical productions as Dramaturg. Alongside her RSC work, she has her own practice as a freelance Dramaturg and New Work Consultant.
TRAINED: Réjane holds two undergraduate degrees, and an MA in Literary Translation (specialising in Theatre) from UEA's prestigious Creative Writing department.
OTHER WORK: Réjane has a background in producing, and has previously worked at the Lyric Hammersmith and The Old Vic.

CHARLOTTE SUTTON CDG
CASTING DIRECTOR

RSC: *All Is But Fantasy, Measure for Measure, Hamlet, Love's Labour's Lost.*
THEATRE INCLUDES: *Guys & Dolls* (Bridge); *The Unfriend* (Wyndham's/Criterion/Chichester Festival Theatre); *The Secret Life of Bees* (Almeida); *Best of Enemies, Death of a Salesman* (Young Vic/West End); *Further than the Furthest Thing, Fairview, The Convert, Trade, Dutchman* (Young Vic); *Our Generation* (Chichester Festival Theatre/National Theatre); *The Inquiry, Assassins, Local Hero, The Famous Five, Sing Yer Heart Out for the Lads, Doubt, Oklahoma!, The Deep Blue Sea, The Watsons, Cock, Flowers for Mrs Harris, The Meeting, Random/Generations, Quiz, Fiddler on the Roof, Strife, Mack and Mabel* (Chichester Festival); *Caroline, or Change* (Chichester Festival Theatre/Hampstead/West End); *South Pacific* (Sadler's Wells/Chichester Festival Theatre/UK tour); *Cock* (Ambassador's); *Company* (Gielgud); *Long Day's Journey into Night* (Wyndham's/BAM/LA); *wonder.land, The Light Princess, Emil and the Detectives, The Elephantom* (National Theatre).
FILM INCLUDES: *Disenchanted* (Walt Disney Studios, UK casting); *Mufasa: The Lion King* (Walt Disney Studios, Taka Cub and Chigaru Casting).

CHRISTOPHER WORRALL CDG
CASTING DIRECTOR
RSC: *All Is But Fantasy, The BFG, Fat Ham*. Christopher is Associate Casting Director at the RSC.
THEATRE INCLUDES: As Casting Director: *Punch* (Nottingham Playhouse/Young Vic/Apollo Theatre); *The Real and Imagined History of The Elephant Man, The Beekeeper of Aleppo, LAVA* (Nottingham Playhouse); *A Streetcar Named Desire, Rock/Paper/Scissors, Chicken Soup* (Sheffield Theatres); *Robin Hood, The Caucasian Chalk Circle* (Rose, Kingston); *Arabian Nights* (Bristol Old Vic); *Assassins* (Chichester Festival Theatre); *The Red Lion* (New Wolsey Theatre); *Sucker Punch* (Queen's Theatre/UK tour); *The Misfortune of the English, Tom Fool, Two Billion Beats* (Orange Tree) and *The Climbers* (Theatre by the Lake). Christopher began his career as Casting Assistant at the Donmar Warehouse.
FILM & TELEVISION INCLUDES: As Casting Associate: *The Choral, Emma, Call the Midwife.*

NIA LYNN
VOICE AND TEXT
RSC: *All Is But Fantasy, The Two Gentlemen of Verona, The School for Scandal, As You Like It, The Alchemist, The Merchant of Venice, A Christmas Truce, Love's Labour's Lost and Won, Wendy & Peter Pan, Matilda The Musical, Oppenheimer* (West End transfer); *Making Mischief, The Mouse and His Child, Antony and Cleopatra, The Winter's Tale* (UK tour); *First Encounters: The Taming of the Shrew, A Mad World My Masters, Beauty and the Beast.*
TRAINED: Guildhall School of Music and Drama, the Royal Central School of Speech and Drama.
THEATRE INCLUDES: *Arcadia* (The Old Vic); *Richard III* (Shakespeare's Globe); *Branwen Dadeni, Tiger Bay* (Wales Millennium Centre); *Watch on the Rhine, Limehouse, The Committee, The Prime of Miss Jean Brodie, Marys Seacole* (Donmar Warehouse); *Middle* (National Theatre); *Galwad* (Welsh National Theatre/Sky Arts); *Dirty Dancing, Bridgerton* (Secret Cinema); *The Night of the Iguana* (West End); *King Hadley II* (Theatre Royal Stratford East); *Tylwyth, Faust + Greta, Macbeth* (Theatre Genedlaethol Cymru); *A Number* (Bridge); *Goat* (Rambert Dance Company); *City of Glass* (Lyric/HOME Manchester); *Milky Peaks* (Theatr Clwyd); *The Complete Deaths* (Spymonkey); *Against Captain's Orders* (Punchdrunk); *My name is Rachel Corrie* (Young Vic).
TELEVISION INCLUDES: *Pride and Prejudice* (Netflix); *Under Salt Marsh* (Sky); *Doctor Who, Boiling Point, Rain Dogs, Steeltown Murders,* CBeebies' *A Midsummer Night's Dream* (BBC); *The Thief, His Wife and the Canoe* (ITV); *Rain Dogs* (HBO); *Dinner with the Parents* (CBS); *Serpent Queen* (Lionsgate); *Tree on a Hill* (BBC Cymru).
FILM INCLUDES: *Back to Black* (Netflix); *Dream Horse* (Sky/Film 4); *The Great Escaper, Save the Cinema* (Sky); *No Way Up* (Independent); *Y Swn* (BBC Cymru).
OTHER: Nia is the Principle Study Jazz Singing Teacher and Honorary Associate at The Royal Academy of Music.

CHRISTOPHER TENDAI
ASSOCIATE CHOREOGRAPHER

RSC: *All Is But Fantasy, Matilda The Musical* **(Cambridge Theatre, West End).**
TRAINED: The Urdang Academy.
THEATRE INCLUDES: *Personality: The Lloyd Price Musical* (Southbank Centre); *Cabaret* (Kit Kat Club/Playhouse Theatre); *Jekyll & Hyde* (Cecil Sharp House); *Carousel, Jesus Christ Superstar* (Regent's Park Open Air Theatre); *Dick Whittington* (National Theatre); *West Side Story* (Manchester Royal Exchange); *Hamilton* (Victoria Palace); *In the Heights* (King's Cross Theatre); *Dirty Dancing* (Secret Cinema); *Damn Yankees* (Clapham Theatre); *Hairspray* (Ireland tour). Resident and Associate Credits: Resident Choreographer & Young Dance Supervisor for *MJ The Musical* (Prince Edward Theatre); Associate Choreographer for *Jesus Christ Superstar* (Australian tour); Resident Choreographer for *Jesus Christ Superstar* (UK tour).
CHOREOGRAPHY INCLUDES: *Beauty and the Beast* (Storyhouse); *A Tribute to DALIDA* (Peacock Theatre); *Soccerbible & Adidas; AiTopia* (Young Vic); *CAKE: The Marie Antoinette Musical* (The Other Palace); *Closer to Heaven* (Turbine Theatre); *Wonderland in Alice* (Theatre Peckham); *Harry & Greta* (New Wolsey Theatre); *MODE* (Elmhurst Ballet Company); *RENT* (Eve Lyon's Studio Theatre); *Carrie* (Bernie Grants Arts Centre); *Guap Gala* (Natural History Museum); *Wuthering Heights* (Turbine Theatre); *iNk'd* (Pegasus Theatre); *Bare: A Pop Opera* (Eve Lyon's Studio Theatre); *Children of Eden* (Union Theatre); *Piano Legends* (UK tour).
TELEVISION INCLUDES: *Blitz* (Apple TV); *The Greatest Dancer, The Kingsman, Strictly Come Dancing* (BBC); *Episodes* (Channel 4); *Brit Awards* (ITV); *Union J* (UK tour); *Fleur East* (Wimbledon Stadium); London Olympics.

MUMBA DODWELL
ASSISTANT DIRECTOR

RSC: *All Is But Fantasy.*
TRAINED: Mumba (she/her) began her directing training on the Intro to Directing course at the Young Vic. She was the 2019/20 recipient of the National Youth Theatre's Bryan Forbes Bursary to train alongside the Rep Company. Mumba is a London-based director and facilitator.
THEATRE INCLUDES: As Director: *The Welkin* (Guildhall School of Music and Drama); *Sense and Sensibility* (Exeter Barnfield Theatre); *Attack of the 50ft Black Woman, Black Ice* (Theatre503); *The Last Black Girl on Earth* (The Last Wood Festival, Roundhouse); *Boy/Girl/Boy/Girl* (Playing Up 2022, National Youth Theatre); *Intimate Apparel* (Guildhall School of Music and Drama); *The Ancestors* (National Youth Theatre/English Heritage); *Great Expectations* (Offie nominated. National Youth Theatre). As Associate/Assistant Director: *London Road, Slave Play* (Noël Coward Theatre, West End); *London Road, Death of England, Othello* (National Theatre); *The Secret Life of Bees, Daddy* (Almeida); *Rockets and Blue Lights* (Royal Exchange Theatre/Lockdown Festival/BBC Radio 3&4/National Theatre); *Othello* (National Youth Theatre/Royal & Derngate/Bolsover Castle); *A Midsummer Night's Dream, Frankenstein* (National Youth Theatre); *The Court Must Have a Queen* (Hampton Court Palace).

THE ROYAL SHAKESPEARE COMPANY

PATRON
His Majesty King Charles III

BOARD
Shriti Vadera
Chair

Andrew Miller MBE
Sir Mark Thompson
Co-Deputy Chairs

Daniel Evans
Tamara Harvey
Co-Artistic Directors

Andrew Leveson
Executive Director

Geoff Barton
Sir Nicholas Hytner
Amanda Parker
Winsome Pinnock
Anna Sedgley
Professor Emma Smith
Jonathan Smith
Professor Ayanna Thompson
Liz Vernon
Susan Tomasky
President RSC America (observer)

The RSC was established in 1961. It is incorporated under Royal Charter and is a registered charity, number 212481.

January 2026

All Is But Fantasy

A musical adaptation.

Music, Lyrics and Book by Whitney White

Time
Now, and always.

Place
A concert venue or rehearsal space where players can roam freely between the worlds of performing and rehearsing music and exploring and presenting text. At other times, Shakespeare's world. And still other spaces of conjuring.

Characters

Woman	a female-identifying performer of the African Diaspora. Lady Macbeth, Emilia, Juliet, and others.
Man	a male-identifying performer. Macbeth, Iago, Romeo and others.
First Witch	a female- or non-binary-identifying performer of the African Diaspora.
Second Witch	a female- or non-binary-identifying performer of the African Diaspora.
Third Witch	a female- or non-binary-identifying performer of the African Diaspora.
Desdemona	a female- or non-binary identifying performer. Desdemona, Juliet and others.
The Band	a collection of geniuses, misfits, and lovers of theatre.

All Is But Fantasy premiered at the Royal Shakespeare Company in 2026.

Prior to the Royal Shakespeare Company premiere as *All Is But Fantasy, Emilia, Juliet,* and *Richard III* were commissioned by the American Repertory Theater at Harvard University [Diane Paulus, Artistic Director, Diane Borger, Executive Producer] and *Lady Macbeth* had its world premiere under the title *Macbeth in Stride*, produced by the American Repertory Theater, and subsequently produced by Shakespeare Theatre Company Washington, DC,

Philadelphia Theatre Company Philadelphia, PA and Brooklyn Academy of Music Brooklyn, NY.

Please note: This version of the script went to press before the performance and so may differ from the final version.

A note:
irreverence is everything.

Find a way to marry Shakespeare's words and contemporary language. Try, and encourage the performers and designers to be present in their full selves at every moment and do not sacrifice that. There is room in the language and music for all of you.

Italics indicate sung, rapped, elevated or spoken in rhythm.

// indicates an interruption or overlap.

A phrase in ((brackets)) comes from an intensely individual point of view.

I. Lady Macbeth

We begin with a prologue. The house is at half but the vibe is full. Whether the audience gets in on the vibe or not, the show is about to go down. A few musicians warm up on stage, tuning their instruments.

*And then a **Woman** comes on stage in contemporary dress. She says hello to them. She isn't overdressed, she knows she will be performing tonight but she is somewhere between rehearsals and a finished thing.*

"If Knowledge Is Power", an RnB song for the ages, floods the space.

Woman
WHAT'S THE DIFFERENCE 'TWEEN WHAT YOU'RE TOLD
AND WHAT YOU KNOW?
WHAT'S THE DIFFERENCE 'TWEEN WHAT YOU'RE TOLD
AND WHAT YOU KNOW?

CAN YOU REALLY REAP WHAT YOU SOW?
PLANT YOUR ROOTS DEEP
OR YOU'LL HAVE NOWHERE TO GROW!

MOTHER SAID TO LOOK BOTH WAYS
HOLD YOUR HEAD UP HIGH.
DON'T SPEAK TOO LOUD
YOU MIGHT GET BY.

SHE SAID, AIM HIGH
HIGH AS THE SKY
BUT BE CAREFUL GIRL
THEY MAY NOT LET YOU BY.

I ASKED WHY?
SHE SAID, THAT'S THE WAY IT GOES
I ASKED WHY?

SHE SAID. . . .
IT'S A STORY EVERYONE KNOWS.

BUT WHAT'S THE DIFFERENCE BETWEEN WHAT
YOU'RE TOLD
AND WHAT YOU KNOW?

> *She falls out of song and relies on her own language.*
> *Her eyes find the audience, she speaks to them.*

Woman
Good evening.
I said good evening.
Sorry to just sing at you like that.
I hope you're alright.
I should at least *ask* if you're alright
before I get into the
—before *we* get into all of the singing and the story
Because once this gets going
Once *these plays* get going, they just sort of . . .

> *She makes a gesture. Flight taking off.*

Shakespearean plays, I mean.
Well *all* plays I guess
but let's just stick to Shakespeare's.
Because I love them.
I will see them on the West End on Broadway
In a regional theater
 . . . oh. I'm an American
technically, I am from "the regions" where we actually do a lot of Shakespeare.
—for us "Americans," regional just means outside of New York
I'm a meager peasant from the Midwest.
The Midwest is one of those regions in which you're supposed to say
Hi, how are you, how ya doing and not just sing at people about what you want.
anyways.

I'll watch these plays. Shakespeare's plays . . . *anywhere*.
Even with children.
Especially with children.
In churches, in community centers . . .
In theaters.
As for theater, this is a beautiful one, isn't it?

Really. Just take a second and take a look around.
Not bad.
Thank you for programming this.
The history here?
the people who have worked and played here?
and really all these people they've all been doing
—we've all been doing
The same plays.
The same *stories*

Beat. She finds an audience member.

Do you know much about how theatre is made?
What do you know about it?
Have you ever tried it before?
It's kinda like sausage.
You know, you want to eat the sausage
 . . . but we don't want to know how the sausage is made.
You know what I'm saying?
I am in the weird part of "theatre-making" where we
perform the show for you all
but we also rehearse it because we're not finished.
So we work on the show in the daytime, like maniacs
trying to change every little thing we can
And then when we perform it for you
While we are performing
we're freaking out about uh, I don't know . . . everything?
And then the next day we *scramble* to fix it
then we do it all again.
it's all very exciting
but it's also like a kind of hell

because people *pay*
Sometimes boo-koo duckets. (That's a lot of money)
to watch you while you're in what can be
quite compromising situations!
You could be naked or kissing, naked and kissing or murdering people
Murdering people while naked . . . you never really know what these directors are gonna make
you do okay?
So it's like a loop. It's limbo, you know and . . .

> *Before she can finish a* **Man** *comes out on stage.*
> *He brings a microphone center and does a few tests.*
> *He also has an accordion, and sits it near the*
> *other instruments.*

Man
Check, Check.
Testing. Testing.
One, two . . .

Woman
Hey . . .

Man
Hi.

Woman
Yeah it's not time for you to // be here.

Man
Oh it's not?

Woman
No. Not // yet.

Man
I mean
I like to—
I need to just warm up a bit. //

Check on things, make sure I'm all set.

Woman
I'm kind of warming up right now. // do you mind if I . . .

Man
Sure. That's okay!

Woman
—I know. // I know it's okay.

Man
I mean.
It's quite good when we're in space together.
It's good for // us.

Woman
Give me a moment. Okay?

Man
alright.
See you in a bit then.

> *Perhaps this is the only bit that hurts his feelings, but he picks up his pride and his instrument and goes.*
> *The* **Woman** *refocuses her attention on the audience.*

Woman
Where was I . . .
—oh my god.
Did you just get excited? Because of him?
You did.
Admit it.
You think he's cute?
Are you a bit relieved he's in the show?
Okay so let me just get this all the way, out of the way
—can you come back please?

> *The* **Man** *runs out again to introduce himself.*

Man
Hi there. Hi, how are you.
I'm (*actor shares their name*)
Nice to be with all of you.

Woman
Tell them who // you're

Man
I'm (*actor shares their name*)
I'll be playing Man and a few other characters.

Woman
—and I am (*actor shares their name*) and will be Woman and a few other characters.
I suppose it's important to say that we've been

Man
We've been working on the plays for a while now

Woman
These plays in which a man and a woman
get married

Man
or fall in love and then get married

Man
or fall in love and die . . .

Man
—or get married and die.

Woman
Over and over again
So we are . . .

Man
We are figuring some things out.

> *Shifting, quickly.*

Is that good?

Woman
Yes, it's good. Thank you.

Man
Okay. See you in a few.

Woman
> (*to audience*)

I started all this
What else is there to say

> *Beat.*

I started all this, looking at these plays
and thinking about what it means for someone like me
to *be* in these plays
To play women in these plays
When I was younger.
and I think I should say that since then, I've lost a few good women in my family.
. . . maybe you have too?
a few Juliets.
A few Emilias
And I'm trying to figure out why.
((Oh god))

> *Beat.*

I might need some help
That can be a hard thing to ask for

And I'm at that age when I'm supposed to be in charge
of . . . things?
Which is truly *terrible*. Do you know what I mean?
I mean adulthood? ack.
. . . dear god . . . I have to be responsible.

for what seems to be . . . like everything.
And I'm supposed to be—

Before she can finish this bit three women enter, each with their own microphone and carrying a sacred object—an object sacred

Woman
—okay. hey.

Witches
Hi babe / wassup /
you ready for us? / almost done? /
seems longer than last time?

Woman
. . . was it? Am I running behind?

First Witch
I mean a little bit.

Second Witch
We just thought we'd come out and help move things along.

Third Witch
—so here we are.

Woman
(*to audience*)
These are the witches y'all.

First Witch
That's a charged term.

Woman
Okay. These are my band members.

Second Witch
Collaborators.

Third Witch
Future replacements.

Second Witch
Would hate for you to break an ankle.

First Witch
—You wrong for that . . .

Woman
—in *Macbeth* there are witches.

First Witch
And if you don't know

All Witches
—now you know.

Woman
So that's where we're going to start.

Third Witch
With us. Hello.

Second Witch
Do we get to do introductions?

Woman
Uhm . . .
Sure.

Third Witch
Play us something fun, yeah?

> *The* **Woman** *strikes up a few major chords or builds a beat for the players to express and introduce themselves. The* **Witches** *introduce themselves in time over the beat.*

Woman
AWWWWWW YEAH!

First Witch
MY NAME IS . . . AND I'M SO SO FLY
I'M FIVE FOOT FIVE AND I'M FEELIN' ALIVE
. . . IS MY ZODIAC SIGN
I'LL BE YOUR FIRST WITCH, TONIGHT.

Second Witch
MY NAME IS . . . AND I'M SO SO FLY
SHAKESPEARE ISN'T REALLY MY MAIN GUY
I'M NORMALLY THE LEAD BUT LET'S SEE ABOUT MISS THING
I'LL BE THE SECOND WITCH TONIGHT.

Third Witch
MY NAME IS . . . AND THE WORLD'S ON FIRE
I SAID MY NAME IS . . . AND THE WORLD'S ON FIRE
I SAID MY NAME IS . . . AND THE WORLD'S ON FIRE
I SAID MY NAME IS . . . AND THE WORLD'S ON FIRE!

Woman
Okayyyyy! Thank you. Thank you to the witches.
Round of applause for them please.
Thank you, thank you.

> *The* **Woman** *leads the applause for a beat and then settles at the lead singer microphone again.*

Woman
So these women.

Second Witch
Weird sisters.

First Witch
—lord, not sisters.

Second Witch
That's what people always call us.

I. Lady Macbeth 15

Woman
These women begin the play
Shakespeare's play
talking.
That's all they're really doing.

> *Lights pull us a hair deeper into what could feel like
> a typical production of* Macbeth. *Underscore: "If
> Knowledge Is Power". Mystery and mood as the three*
> **Witches** *draw closer to each other. The* **Woman** *watches
> them from afar.*

First Witch
When shall we three meet again
In thunder lightning or in rain?

Second Witch
When the hurly burly's done.
When the battle's lost and won

First Witch
That will be ere the set of sun.

All
A drum, a drum, Macbeth doth come.

Woman
—and so we started talking.
because a lot of this
A lot of doing these plays
is figuring out how to do them.

> *The* **Women** *change their physical arrangement, they
> make themselves a hair more comfortable, gathering closer,
> speaking to each other and the audience. Underscoring
> returns to a dark version of "If Knowledge Is Power".*

First Witch
Motherhood.

Second Witch
Childhood.

Third Witch
Sex.

First Witch
Society.

Second Witch
Who's in power?

Third Witch
Who's in charge?

Woman
Someone pushed me in the street the other day.

First Witch
—Cut me in the queue.

Second Witch
Next time, push them back!

Third Witch
Don't do that.

Second Witch
Didn't get the job.

Woman
Mother's sick . . .

First Witch
—Mother's dead.

Third Witch
Doctor didn't listen.

I. Lady Macbeth 17

Woman
It happened to me too.

Second Witch
It happened to *mine*, too

Woman
    (*to audience*)
We told each other stories of things we've been told
and things we know
I told them my story.
And they told me theirs.
They told me

Second Witch
once upon a time.

First Witch
maybe your prince will come

Second Witch
He ain't coming.

Third Witch
the wedding ring.

All
the glass ceiling

Woman
—*Those* are the stories that are told to us
from crib to grave.
"Ra ra" feminism! the second and the third wave . . .
    (*to audience*)
But if you think that all those stories didn't worm their way
into your brain?
 . . . you think them narratives ain't doing thangs?
to you?

to me?
to us?

First Witch
—But *us?* ain't really *us*.

Woman
True.

First Witch
We're talking about the Black us.

Witches and Woman
Well!

Woman
The brown us.

Witches
okay!

Second Witch
The femme us.

All
Push through!

Woman
The queer us.
for those of *us* our stories go a little more like:

Witches and Woman
Lil' sister don't go too far
The man is watching, don't be no star
do the best with what you have
work twice as hard, might still get had!

Woman
and that's how Shakespeare wrote it.
 . . . That's how the movies show it . . .
and it snakes its way through our lives
because wanting too much is a *condition*.

First Witch
—disease.

Woman
The Lady Macbeth—

Third Witch
Shaking, sweating—

Woman
oooh!!!

First Witch
Wait a minute
Wait a minute miss thang . . .

> *At some point, the women began to move about the space again. This time with precious objects, libation, placing fruits about the space, and a modest sage stick. They work together to prepare the space.*

Woman
What are you—
Are you doing a spell?

First Witch
Maybe.

Second Witch
—depends.

First Witch
What do you want?

Woman
Excuse me?

First Witch
I said, what do you want?

Woman
You want me to just cut to it?

First Witch
Please!

> **Second Witch**
> of course.

Third Witch
don't let it be a secret.

> **First Witch**
> we have so much to do.

Second Witch
so yes.

Woman
I can say anything?

First Witch
Reclaim honey . . .

All
Reclaaaaaim!

Woman
Is this a sisterhood?

Witches
Could be.

I. Lady Macbeth   21

Woman
Alright then sister-enemy-witch-friends . . .
I want . . .

> *Underscoring shifts to the root chord of "Reach for It"
> revving us up for the song.*

Woman
Power.

First Witch
> (*cutting off the* **Band**)

Can you do a little better than that?

Woman
No, for real for real.
Power.
Capital P.

First Witch
—and?

Woman
a voice.

Second Witch
—that's easy.

Woman
a choice

All Witches
—and?

> *The* **Witches** *are finally pleased and allow her to
> continue. Underscoring returns, deepening, spreading into
> light solos and riffs.*

Woman
LifeRightsPursuitHappiness
Don't touch my hair

Don't talk when I'm talking

Don't cut me in line.
Don't make me wait
Don't promise me something
And take everything away.
Don't assume I can't feel pain
Don't say there's too much on my plate
Don't get the white man on my case

Witches
Yup / yes.

keep going / come on /
let's go

Witches
—and?

Woman
I dunno.
That's kind of a lot.

Second Witch
But what is behind the want?

Woman
I guess
I want to understand . . .

Third Witch
Understand what?

Woman
—the story.
I want to understand the story.

First Witch
Close enough.
Okay now everybody close your eyes
　　(*to audience*)

I'm serious do it
WE CAN SEE YOU
close your eyes
Let the vibes in
Take the time
Take the breath.
And let's breathe together
    (*to* **Woman**)
And you . . .

Woman
Yes?

First Witch
can you go put on something a little more . . . *Macbeth*?

Woman
Of course.

First Witch
Thank you.

> *With a snap lights fall to mystery. Our rehearsal space is now a performance space. The **Witches** fall into a song as their ritual takes over the space. The **Woman** watches, learns, and tries to find her place.*
>
> *The women make use of their sacred objects and begin to move about, incanting. Invoking. One wields an incense stick. Another takes a sip of rum. Other ritual or personal objects can be used in this prologue, totems that root and center the players.*

Witches
Come on in, come on down.
There is no up there is no down.
By the pricking of my thumbs,
Something wicked this way comes . . .

*And then the three **Witches** snap their fingers and our **Band** enters. They sit to play and music shifts to a Hallelujah cycle, dark and patient.*

As they sing they incant more. They bless the space, musicians and each other.

All

Hallelujah!
    Hallelujah!
Hallelujah!
    Hallelujah!

> *The **Woman** enters again, processing her way downstage as close to the audience as she can get, taking her place at the "lead singer" microphone.*
>
> *There is something darkly utilitarian to her clothes, and now that she completes the ensemble they all come together.*
>
> *The **Band** vamps underneath, weaving around her text and dipping low when she commands. For the rest of the evening the music and story will be one.*

Woman

    (*to audience*)
Okay, I'm back.
Here we go y'all, here we go!
Let's just get into it.
Let's just climb all the way in and down
into her.
Into Lady Macbeth.

First Witch
That's right.

Woman
She was the first, my first
My first love, in these plays.
I remember where I was when I first read her lines.
I remember how she made me feel

I. Lady Macbeth

Second Witch
So let's get into it.

> **Third Witch**
> let's do it.

>> **First Witch**
>> Let's go!

First Witch
We got the lights and the band and the people

Third Witch
That's y'all

Woman
and we've got the story
Her story.

Woman
One, two, three, four . . .

Song 2: Reach for It

Woman
WHEN I CLOSE MY EYES I SEE EXACTLY
JUST WHAT I NEED
WHEN I CLOSE MY EYES I SEE IT
RIGHT IN FRONT OF ME
THE WAY THAT IT GOES POWER'S NOT SUPPOSED
TO LOOK LIKE ME

BUT I NEED	**Witches, Man, Band**
I NEED WHAT I NEED	AHHHHHH

WHERE HAVE ALL THE GOOD MEN GONE

I SWEAR I'M LOOKING JUST
FOR ONE, FOR ONE . . .
HANG THE LIARS ONE
BY ONE BY ONE BY ONE

Witches
HANG THE LIARS ONE
BY ONE BY ONE BY ONE

IF I CAN'T FIND ONE,
THEN I'LL MAKE ONE
I'LL CUT HIM FROM STONE,
I'LL MAKE HIM A KING
BUT A QUEEN,
OH, WHERE IS SHE?

Witches
QUEEN . . . SHE

Woman
WHAT IF I REACH FOR IT

Witches, Man, Band
REACH FOR IT

REACH FOR IT
JUST TO TASTE IT

Witches
AHHHHHH

JUST TO TOUCH IT
FOR AN INCH OF IT
FOR AN INCH OF IT

Witches, Man, Band
AHHHHHH

*The **Women** vocalize together, finding more intersecting harmonies, riffs, and as they do their physical movement grows. They have a proper dance break.*

Second Witch
WE WON'T KNOW WHEN WE'LL EVER MEET AGAIN . . .

> **Woman, First Witch, Third Witch**
> *DON'T KNOW. NO WE DON'T KNOW.*

Third Witch
WE DON'T KNOW IF SIN IS EVEN REALLY EVEN SIN

Witches, Woman, Man, Band
SO IF FOUL IS FAIR THEN FAIR IS FOUL
AMBITION'S NOT A SIN AT ALL!

Woman
BUT A QUEEN . . . OH WHERE IS SHE?

I. Lady Macbeth   27

Woman
WHAT IF I REACH FOR IT
REACH FOR IT
JUST TO TASTE IT
JUST TO TOUCH IT
FOR AN INCH OF IT
FOR AN INCH OF IT!

Witches, Man
REACH FOR IT
AHHHHHH

Woman, Second Witch
WHAT IF I REACH FOR IT
REACH FOR IT
JUST TO TASTE IT
JUST TO TOUCH IT
FOR AN INCH OF IT
FOR AN INCH OF IT!

All
AHHHHHHH
REACH FOR IT
AHHHHHHH
AHHHHHHH

Woman
A DRUM A DRUM MACBETH DOTH COME!

Woman and Witches
A DRUM A DRUM MACBETH DOTH COME
A DRUM A DRUM MACBETH DOTH COME
A DRUM A DRUM MACBETH DOTH COME!

All
A DRUM A DRUM MACBETH DOTH COME
A DRUM A DRUM MACBETH DOTH COME
A DRUM A DRUM MACBETH DOTH COME

Woman
A DRUM A DRUM MACBETH DOTH COME!

>*Somehow when we finish this—we are Lady Macbeth*

>*The **Women** finish the song with power. The **Second Witch** steps apart pushing them into the story again. The other witches follow her.*

Second Witch
Okay you want to get into her story?
. . . because that's your story. Right?
then, he's coming.

Woman
. . . He?
Which he?

Second Witch
The "he"

Third Witch
Chile, all he's

First Witch
The "man".

Second Witch
The "lead".

All Witches
The king to be.

Woman
I don't mind a he.

Second Witch
What about a white he?

Woman
Does it have to be?

Witches
I mean . . .

First Witch
—In these plays?

Witches
usually.

Woman
—who says there has to be a he?

> The **Band** *supplies a lush major chord. The* **Witches** *each respond on a note in the chord.*

Second Witch
Time.

Third Witch
Space.

First Witch
The world.

Witches
The bible.

    Woman
    —wait a minute y'all—

Second Witch
Every story.

Third Witch
Every movie.

First Witch
Every play—
Like *allllllllllll* the plays.

Woman
So
Woman . . . must choose
Between her own story and—

Second Witch
(losing patience)
Ugh. Is this evening really gonna be all about *her*?
Why do you get to stand in front of all of us
and look all cute and take up space?

First Witch
You gon' rework a bunch of 400-year-old plays just
for your ego?

Woman
Yup.
Sure did! Sure did!

Third Witch
Why?
When so many of us don't get what we deserve?

Woman
you're right.
(focusing on the audience)
It's not about me.
It's about she—*her*
Y'all and that lady in right there in aisle three.
It's about your daughter, your daughter's friend
every woman whose story met an untimely end
and all of Shakespeare's great women
who never seem to make it out of these plays alive!

Beat.

But for now, can we just start with me because we're here
I'm in costume, it's going great?

Third Witch
Then you need him.
Because there is no story without him.

I. Lady Macbeth   31

Woman
Fine.
But how does the play start?
For her.
For her character?
if we flip it
how does *her* story start?

Third Witch
—her story starts . . . with a letter.

> *The* **Third Witch** *draws closer, handing her a letter as the* **Man** *appears in silhouette. He holds an instrument—one which he will play off and on throughout the rest of the show. This can be an accordion, a guitar . . . whatever he is excellent in. Underscoring rumbles on a low Rubato.*

Man
They met me in the day . . .

Woman and Man
of success

Man
—and I have learn'd by the perfect'st report, they have more in them than mortal knowledge. When I burnt in desire to question them further, they made themselves air, into which they vanish'd—whiles I stood rapt in the wonder of it, came missives from the King who all-hail'd me "Thane of Cawdor," by which title, before, these weïrd sisters saluted me and referred me to the coming on of time with—

Man/Witches
"Hail, King that shalt be!"

> *The* **Witches** *snap their fingers again and underscoring shifts to "Dark World". As they vocalize the* **Man** *enters, making his way to the lead microphone which up until this point has been the* **Woman***'s. He is every rocker's dream.*

There is no warmth, there is no accommodation. Just being. The two collide for a moment.

Song 3: Dark World

Man
IT WAS A DARK WORLD
WHEN WE MET
WE WERE BORN, WE WERE
BORN TO IT.
BEFORE WE SET FOOT ON
THIS EARTH IT WAS ABLAZE

IT WAS ABLAZE . . .

KING AND QUEEN AND
SYSTEMS REIGN
WE WILL FALL, WE WILL
FALL INTO IT
I CAN BE KING THAT'S
WHAT THEY SAY
CAN WE MAKE, CAN WE
MAKE IT?

Witches
STAY ON TRACK
RUN IT BACK

HE AIN'T ALL THAT!

Woman
HE KIND OF WAS?

Witches
—GET IT RIGHT

Witches
OOHHHHH

Witches/Woman
WHAT CAN WE DO TO
PUT THE FIRE OUT?
OOHHHHHH

THEY MUST FALL!
THEY MUST FALL!
WE CAN WE DO,

HOW CAN WE CHANGE
IT?

Woman
   (*ad lib*)
WHAT CAN WE DO TO
PUT THE FIRE OUT?

I. Lady Macbeth   33

Man
DOWN IS UP, AND UP
IS DOWN
FOUL IS FAIR AND FAIR
IS FOUL
COME WHAT MAY,
THEY CAN DO THEIR
WORST
I DON'T CARE CAUSE
YOU'RE THE GROUND

Witches
OOO

Woman
WHAT CAN WE DO TO
PUT THE FIRE OUT?

Man
TAKE WHAT YOU WANT
TAKE WHAT YOU NEED
TO GET A LEG UP
THERE ARE NO
BAD DEEDS

Witches
OOHHHH

BAD DEEDS, AHHH.

Man
AND IF THE WORLD
GOES MAD
LET IF FALL, LET IT FALL
WE DON'T NEED
ANYTHING AT ALL
LET THE BLOOD FLOW
IF IT MUST, THEN IT MUST
WE'LL SURVIVE IT ALL!
'CAUSE YOU'RE THE
GROUND
YOU'RE THE GROUND

Woman, Witches
WORLD GOES MAD

AHHHHH
ANYTHING AT ALL.

AHHHHH

OHHHHH

Woman
IT'S A DARK WORLD!

Man
YOU'RE THE GROUND

Witches
DARK WORLD
DARK WORLD
DARK WORLD

Man
YOU'RE THE GROUND!

Man
I CAN BE KING THAT'S
WHAT THEY SAY
CAN WE MAKE, CAN WE
MAKE IT?
I CAN BE KING THAT'S
WHAT THEY SAY
CAN WE MAKE, CAN
WE MAKE IT?

Woman
WHAT CAN WE DO TO
PUT THE FIRE OUT?

*With the song's finish the **Man** lingers a breath finishing the letter. He speaks into the **Woman**'s ear.*

Man
This have I thought good to deliver thee
My dearest partner of greatness
Lay it to thy heart, and—

Man and Woman
farewell.

*He is gone. The **Woman** calls the **Witches** back. She looks to the spot he once stood in, now vacant.*

Woman
Not bad.
Macbeth looks good on him.

First Witch
that's the point

I. Lady Macbeth

Woman Witches And he's going to be king? mm hmm. if he's going to be king Than that means I'm gonna be—
(building a rhythm and moment of play)

	Witches
I'm gonna be, I'm gonna be	*You're gonna be, You're gonna be . . .*
I'm gonna be, I'm gonna be . . .	*You're gonna be, You're gonna be . . .*

Second Witch
Can we focus? Ambition. King. Queen.
What are you gonna do to make it happen?

Woman
I'm focused I just—wait
Why not just give power directly to me?

All Witches
    (laughing)
Oh honey . . . / come now

First Witch
—Because that's the way the world works honey
Lady MacB hitches her cart to his
So that's it. That's marriage.
unless you want to change the story

Woman
—but

36 All Is But Fantasy

Second Witch
Okay then.
Speak the words.
Her words.

> *Underscoring rises on the root chord of "Reach for It" as the **Woman** falls to Shakespeare's language, addressing the audience.*

Woman
He is my husband—

Third Witch
Macbeth.

Woman
—Glamis . . .

First Witch
Glamis thou art,

Second Witch
. . . and?

Woman
   (*falling to Shakespeare*)
and Cawdor; and shalt be
What thou art promised:

>   *Beat.*

yet do I fear thy nature;
It is too full o' the milk of human kindness
To catch the nearest way: thou wouldst be great;
Art not without ambition, but without
The illness should attend it: what thou wouldst highly,
That wouldst thou holily; wouldst not play false,

And yet wouldst wrongly win: thou'ldst have, great Glamis,
That which cries 'Thus thou must do, if thou have it;
And that which rather thou dost fear to do
Than wishest should be undone.
Hie thee hither
That I may pour my spirits in thine ear;
And chastise thee with the valour of my tongue
All that impedes thee from the golden round
Which fate and metaphysical aid doth seem
To have thee crown'd withal.

> *The pianist plays the opening to "Doll House," a driving, contemplative ballad that changes the mood and makes way for the next song.*

Woman
In the play
you meet Lady Macbeth for two seconds
and then it's *all* about him.
What she's going to do about him.
His nature.
What he's capable of.
—but what about what *she's* capable of?

> *Beat.*
> *She becomes smaller.*

As early as I can remember
I was told there had to be a he and a she.
That life would be very hard without a he.
My mother,
—my incredible mother—
Went at life with no he.
And while she somehow found a way to give me everything.
There was a price.
She has her peace
But there was a price.

Song 4: Doll House

Woman
THE BEST TOY I HAD, IT WAS A DOLL
A LITTLE GIRL, A MAN A HOUSE THEY HAD IT ALL
I MADE THEM TALK I MADE THEM PLAY
THEY HAD A HOME, THEY FOUND THEIR WAY.

> *At the end of this ballad lights pull us into a more naturalistic world. The* **Woman** *speaks to the audience. Perhaps she contemplates the letter that was given to her before as she finds a way back into the story.*

Woman
What happens when a woman—

Second Witch
A *Black* woman

Woman
What happens when a *Black* woman's only way out—

Second Witch
—Up

Woman
What happens when a Black woman's only way *up*—is by violent means?

First Witch
Is violence worse on a Black woman?

Second Witch
The look of it? The feel of it?

Woman
So let me ask you a question:

I. Lady Macbeth 39

Third Witch
—Women, queer folk, and *othered* people out there?

Woman
What are you willing to do to get what you need?
To get what you want?

Second Witch
What are you trying to say?

First Witch
What do you *want?*

Third Witch
What happens in the story?

Woman
In the story
Lady Macbeth gets that letter
And then she just—
She makes an impossible leap to get the power she needs.
So I'm wondering how to do that.

Second Witch
Just leap.

> *The* **Witches** *gesture toward the piano, challenging the* **Woman** *to summon her courage through music. The* **Woman** *makes her way to the piano and for the first time, plays.*
>
> *As she does, the* **Witches** *find a shape of prayer on the ground near the piano and deepen their breathing. The* **Woman** *plays "In the Place of Love" —a chamber song.*

Song 5: In the Place of Love

Woman
IN THE PLACE OF LOVE
LORD LIFT ME UP

MAY I NEVER BE SMALL
MAY I NEVER BE LOST

IN THE PLACE OF LOVE
IN THE PLACE OF LOVE
MAY WHAT COMES OUR WAY   **Witches**
    NEVER TOUCH US!   US

Woman, Witches, Man, Band
OOH!
OOH!
OOH!
AH!

> *The music intensifies, the* **Band** *joins in. The* **Witches** *find their feet, offering their support. Through movement it becomes clear that we are slipping deeper into the spiritual. Channelling, their bodies rock, roll and hands are laid on each other.*

Woman
LORD LIFT ME, LIFT ME, LIFT ME UP
LIFT ME, LIFT ME, LIFT ME UP
LIFT ME, LIFT ME, LIFT ME UP
LIFT ME, LIFT ME, LIFT ME UP! (LORD)

Woman, Witches, Man, Band
LIFT ME, LIFT ME, LIFT ME UP
LIFT ME, LIFT ME, LIFT ME UP

—RAISE MY FACE **UP** OUT OF THE MUD!

LORD LIFT ME, LIFT ME, LIFT ME UP!
LIFT ME, LIFT ME, LIFT ME UP!
LIFT ME, LIFT ME, LIFT ME UP!
LIFT ME, LIFT ME, LIFT ME UP! (LORD)

LORD LIFT ME LIFT ME LIFT ME UP
LIFT ME LIFT ME LIFT ME UP

GIVE ME STRENGTH BEFORE I'M **DUST!**

I. Lady Macbeth   41

With this final lyric the **Woman** *lifts her arm, asking for her microphone again. A* **Witch** *hands it to her and she leaps into the Raven speech. This is a moment of revivalism, and call and response.*

WOMAN
GIVE IT TO ME   COME ON
GIVE IT TO ME   COME ON
GIVE ME . . .

—The raven himself is hoarse
That croaks the fatal entrance of Duncan
Under my battlements. Come, you spirits
That tend on mortal thoughts
Unsex me here.

> *A glimmer from the band and a descant from* **First Witch**

And fill me from the crown to the toe top-full
Of direst cruelty! make thick my blood;

> *More sound. Rising a bit . . .*

Stop up the access and passage to remorse,	**First Witch**
That no compunctious visitings of nature	*Oh!*

Shake my fell purpose, nor keep peace between
The effect and it!

> *More sound!*

	Witches	
Come to my woman's breasts, And take my milk for gall, you murdering ministers,	*Give me*	*Go on ahead*
Wherever in your sightless substances	*Give me*	*Go on and leap*

You wait on nature's mischief!
I said come on!
I said come on!

I said ***come on*** *. . . thick night,*

And pall thee in the dunnest smoke of hell,
That's right / Let it use you!
That my keen knife see not the
wound it makes,
Nor heaven peep through the blanket of the dark,
To cry 'Hold, hold!'

Hold!

> *On her final "Hold" the women lurch back into a very nasty ring shout version of "In the Place of Love". We should feel like we are flowing through the idiom of Black spiritual music from gentle gospel to rock and soul.*

Witches, Man, Band
LORD LIFT ME, LIFT ME, LIFT ME UP
LIFT ME, LIFT ME, LIFT ME UP
LIFT ME, LIFT ME, LIFT ME UP
LIFT ME, LIFT ME, LIFT ME UP! (LORD)

LIFT ME, LIFT ME, LIFT ME UP
LIFT ME, LIFT ME, LIFT ME UP

—RAISE MY FACE **UP** OUT OF THE MUD!

> *The* **Witches** *begin to circle her, and with tambourines build an intense rhythm.*

Woman
   (*to audience*)
I'm talking to you and you, and even you.
All of you out there. To everyone who ever was
and ever will be.
to the *universe*
I'm callin' from the deepest part of me
Say it with me—
Say it with me—

Woman
THERE IS NO DOWN
THERE IS NO DOWN

I. Lady Macbeth 43

THERE IS NO DOWN
THERE IS NO DOWN!

All
THERE IS NO DOWN
THERE IS NO DOWN
THERE IS NO DOWN
THERE IS NO DOWN

Woman
THERE IS NO GROUND!
THERE IS NO GROUND!
THERE IS NO GROUND!
THERE IS NO GROUND!

All
THERE IS NO GROUND!
THERE IS NO GROUND!
THERE IS NO GROUND!
THERE IS NO GROUND!

Woman
LET ME JUST START OVER
NEED ME A NEW DRESS, AND THE
THE FINEST GOWNS

Second Witch
FANCY FOOD AND THE
FASTEST CAR . . .

Third Witch
CAN'T TAKE IT WITH YOU

Woman And Third Witch
BUT, I AM A STAR.

Woman	
I NEED ANOTHER SHOT	**Witches**
ONE MORE ROUND	AH OOH

NOT PLAYIN FAIR THIS TIME   **Witches**
THERE IS NO GROUND!   AH OOH

Woman
THERE IS NO DOWN
THERE IS NO DOWN
THERE IS NO DOWN
THERE IS NO DOWN

All
THERE IS NO DOWN
THERE IS NO DOWN
THERE IS NO DOWN
THERE IS NO DOWN

Woman
THERE IS NO GROUND!
THERE IS NO GROUND!
THERE IS NO GROUND!
THERE IS NO GROUND!

All
THERE IS NO GROUND!
THERE IS NO GROUND!

> *Underscore shifts to a rubato as* **Woman** *finds center stage again.*

Woman
I SAID WHEN I WAKE UP IN THE MORNING
AND I NEED TO REACH FOR IT.
I WILL REACH FOR HIM
BECAUSE I NEED HIM
I NEED HIM.

I NEED ...

> *On the last line, the* **Woman** *uses her voice in a new way. She sings a full operatic sound that rings through the space as she makes her way again to the piano.*

With a gesture she summons the **Man**, *who appears in a different space, contemplating the prophecy given to him. Underscore shifts to a soulful 6/8 feel.*

Woman
I NEED HIM!
JUST COME AND HOLD ME, HOLD ME!
ONE, TWO, THREE, FOUR . . .

She counts the **Band** *back into 4/4, seamlessly drags us, the audience, and* **Band** *back into a revivalist gospel.*

Witches, Man	**Woman**
LORD LIFT ME, LIFT ME,	LIFT ME UP GOD!
LIFT ME UP	
LIFT ME, LIFT ME, LIFT ME UP	LIFT ME UP NOW!
LIFT ME, LIFT ME, LIFT ME UP	
LIFT ME, LIFT ME, LIFT ME UP! (LORD)	

LIFT ME, LIFT ME, LIFT ME UP
LIFT ME, LIFT ME, LIFT ME UP
—GIVE ME STRENGTH . . .

Woman
I said give me strength before I am . . .

All
DUST!

With this the **Man** *finds her, Finally together in the same space and time, the pair embrace. The song finishes fully. The* **Witches** *take a break of sorts. Their opinion of the* **Man** *and* **Woman** *together is complex and varied. Some of us love love, and others would rather rehearsal to continue without the leads subjecting the room to their displays of affection.*

Woman
Hi, how are you—

Man
—fine and you?

Woman
I missed you.

Man
I missed you too.

Woman
    (*falling to Shakespeare*)
Thy letters have transported me beyond this ignorant present, and I feel now
The future in the instant.

Man
Duncan comes here tonight

Woman
And when goes he hence?

Man
Tomorrow.

Woman
O, never
Shall sun that morrow see!

Man
Never shall sun that morrow see?

Woman
. . . yeah . . .

Man
Wait what does that mean?

Woman
They told you that you were going to be king, right?

Witches
We did!   **Man**
                    They did.

Woman
And Duncan is already a king, right?

Witches
That's true . . .   **Man**
                    That's true

Woman
so we gotta . . .

Man
—we gotta what?

Woman
I'm pretty sure
we're gonna have to kill him.

Witches
We didn't say all that!

Woman
    (*falling to Shakespeare*)
—Your face, my thane, is as a book where men
May read strange matters—

Man
Yeah.

Woman
To beguile the time,
Look like the time; bear welcome in your eye,
Your hand, your tongue: look like the innocent flower,
But be the serpent under't. He that's coming
Must be provided for: and you shall put

This night's great business into my dispatch;
Which shall to all our nights and days to come
Give solely sovereign sway and masterdom.

Man
We will speak further

Woman
Only look up clear, babe
To alter favor ever is to fear:
Leave all the rest to me.

> *The* **Women** *prepare themselves and the space for a bit of a party. They give out a few party favors: a bit of garland, sparkle, a bottle of champagne, and a few trinkets and favors that make even the saltiest of artists smile, if even for a moment.*

Song 6: If Knowledge Is Power / Reach for It (Reprises)

Second Witch
AWWW YEAH!!!

WHAT'S THE DIFFERENCE 'TWEEN WHAT
YOU'RE TOLD
AND WHAT YOU KNOW?

Witches
YOU BETTTA GET GET GET IT RIGHT!

Second Witch
WHAT'S THE DIFFERENCE 'TWEEN
WHAT YOU'RE TOLD
AND WHAT YOU KNOW?

Witches
—COME ON THE TIME IS RIGHT!

I. Lady Macbeth 49

Second Witch
CAN YOU REALLY REAP WHAT YOU SOW?
PLANT YOUR ROOTS DEEP
OR YOU'LL HAVE NOWHERE TO GROW!

Witches
WHAT YOU SOW

WHAT YOU SOW

Witches
REACH FOR IT
REACH FOR IT . . .

> *The **Man** plays an instrument loudly, aggressively interrupting the **Witches**.*

Woman
The king has almost supped.
Why have you left the chamber?

Man
We will proceed no further in this business
He hath honored me of late, and I have bought
Golden Opinions from all sorts of people
Which would be worn now in their newest gloss
Not cast aside so soon.

Woman
Was the hope drunk
Wherein you dress'd yourself?
hath it slept since?
And wakes it now, to look so green and pale
At what it did so freely? From this time
Such I account thy love. Art thou afeard
To be the same in thine own act and valour
As thou art in desire?
Wouldst thou have that which thou esteem'st the ornament of life,
And live a coward in thine own esteem,
Letting 'I dare not' wait upon 'I would,'

50   All Is But Fantasy

Like the poor cat i' the adage?
    (*to the* **Witches** *and* **Band**)
Play my song please?

Witches
AWWW YEAH!

Woman
WHAT'S THE DIFFERENCE 'TWEEN WHAT YOU'RE TOLD
AND WHAT YOU KNOW?

        Witches, Band
        YOU BETTTA GET GET GET IT
        RIGHT

Woman
WHAT'S THE DIFFERENCE 'TWEEN
WHAT YOU'RE TOLD
AND WHAT YOU KNOW?

        Witches, Band
        COME ON THE TIME IS RIGHT !

Woman	**Witches, Band**
CAN YOU REALLY REAP	WHAT YOU SOW
WHAT YOU SOW?	
PLANT YOUR ROOTS DEEP	WHAT YOU SOW
OR YOU'LL HAVE NOWHERE	
TO GROW!	

Woman, Witches, Band
REACH FOR IT
REACH FOR IT . . .

Woman, Witches
EYE OF TOAD AND ALL THAT SHIT
TWIGS SNAPPED, AND A LITTLE SPIT
MAMA'S SMILE AND DADDY'S BLACK
A LIL GREASE AND SOME BLOOD

I. Lady Macbeth 51

Third Witch	**Woman, First and Second Witch**
WE'RE CALLIN' OUT!	AND SOME BLOOD...
CALLIN' OUT!	AND SOME BLOOD...
	AND SOME BLOOD...

*The **Man** reaches breaking point. He halts the moment again, this time grabbing the **Woman**'s microphone from her. A true moment of conflict between the two.*

Man
Prithee peace!
I dare do all that may become a man
Who dares do more is none.

Woman
What beast was't, then,
That made you break this enterprise to me?
When you durst do it, then you were a man;
And, to be more than what you were, you would
Be so much more the man. Nor time nor place
Did then adhere, and yet you would make both:
They have made themselves, and that their fitness now
Does unmake you. I have given suck, and know
How tender 'tis to love the babe that milks me:
I would while it was smiling in my face,
Have pluck'd my nipple from his boneless gums,
And dash'd the brains out, had I so sworn as you
Have done to this.

Man
If we should fail?

Woman
We fail!
But screw your courage to the sticking-place,
And we'll not fail.

They move closer. The **Woman** *points to his instrument finally asking him to be a part of the* **Band**.

Woman
WHEN YOU CLOSE YOUR EYES TELL ME
WHAT DO YOU SEE?

Man
I SEE I SEE . . .

Woman
THE WAY THAT IT GOES
I JUST NEED WHAT I NEED

Man
I SEE I SEE..

Woman
REACH FOR IT—

Woman, Man
REACH FOR IT
REACH FOR IT
REACH FOR IT!

The tempo of the music quickens as the **Woman** *and* **Witches** *conjure a bit of an uptempo bop. The* **Woman** *nears the* **Man** *as they all find courage to carry out what's to be done.*

Song 7: Double Double Toil and Trouble

Woman	**Witches**
When Duncan is asleep— Whereto the rather shall his day's hard journey	DOUBLE DOUBLE TOIL AND TROUBLE

I. Lady Macbeth   53

soundly invite him—   DOUBLE DOUBLE TOIL
                                  AND TROUBLE

his two chamberlains
Will I with wine and   DOUBLE DOUBLE TOIL
wassail so convince   AND TROUBLE
That memory, the
warder of the brain,
Shall be a fume, and   DOUBLE DOUBLE TOIL
the receipt of reason   AND TROUBLE

A limbeck only: when in swinish sleep
Their drenched natures lie as in a death,
What cannot you and I perform upon
The unguarded Duncan?
What not put upon his spongy officers,
who shall bear the guilt
Of our great quell?

> *The stage is bathed in a rich red light and we fall into "Double Double Toil and Trouble", a fierce pop number that lets the women congeal into the deadly girl-group they were meant to be.*

Witches
   (*spoken rhythmically*)
DOUBLE DOUBLE TOIL AND TROUBLE
BETTER GIT IT BETTER GIT IT
GIRL ON THE DOUBLE!
DOUBLE DOUBLE TOIL AND TROUBLE
BETTER GIT IT BETTER GIT IT
YOU BETTER KILL THAT MOTHER!
        HUP!

                                        Woman
DOUBLE DOUBLE TOIL AND TROUBLE   OOOO
BETTER GIT IT BETTER GIT IT
GIRL ON THE DOUBLE!

DOUBLE DOUBLE TOIL AND TROUBLE
BETTER GIT IT BETTER GIT IT
YOU BETTER KILL THAT MOTHER!
        HUP!

Woman
I LIKE HIS SHOES
I LIKE HIS WINE
I LIKE THE THRONE
IT SHOULD BE MINE

GOT MY BABY	**Witches**
GOT MY MIND	AH OOH
I GOT MY GOOD KNIFE	AH OOH
THE NIGHT IS MINE	AH OOH

Witches
   (*sung*)
DOUBLE DOUBLE TOIL AND TROUBLE
BETTER GIT IT BETTER GIT IT
GIRL ON THE DOUBLE!

DOUBLE DOUBLE TOIL AND TROUBLE
BETTER GIT IT BETTER GIT IT
YOU BETTER KILL THAT MOTHER!
        HUP!

Woman
WHO'S THIS MAN?
SOME OLD KING?
TELLIN' ME WHAT'S WHAT?
HE'S GOT TO BLEED.

IF ONE MORE MAN	**Witches**
SAYS WHAT'S UP AND DOWN	AH OOH
I'LL CUT HIM EAR TO EAR	AH OOH
TURN THAT SMILE TO A FROWN!	AH OOH

Witches
   (*sung*)
DOUBLE DOUBLE TOIL AND TROUBLE
BETTER GIT IT BETTER GIT IT
GIRL ON THE DOUBLE!

I. Lady Macbeth

DOUBLE DOUBLE TOIL AND TROUBLE
BETTER GIT IT BETTER GIT IT
YOU BETTER KILL THAT MOTHER
      HUP!

Woman
That which hath made them drunk hath made me bold;
What hath quench'd them hath given me fire.

> *An angular, shrieking sound from percussion and guitar startles her.*

Woman
Hark! Peace!
It was the owl that shriek'd, the fatal bellman, which gives
the stern'st good-night. He is about
it: The doors are open; and the surfeited grooms
Do mock their charge with snores: I have drugg'd
their possets,
That death and nature do contend about them, Whether
they live or die. Let's go.

> *She commands the **Band** to play again and underscoring resumes.*

Woman	**Witches**
OOH, YES	THAT'S RIGHT
I LIKE HIS—!!	THAT'S RIGHT

Woman
    (*cutting off the music again*)
Alack, I am afraid they have awaked,
And 'tis not done. The attempt and not the deed
confounds us.
Hark! I laid their daggers ready; He could not miss 'em.
Had he not resembled
My father as he slept, I had done't.
one, two three, four!

Witches	**Woman**

(*rapping*)
DOUBLE DOUBLE DOUBLE AND
TOIL AND TROUBLE BITCH   OOOH!
DOUBLE DOUBLE DOUBLE TOIL
AND TROUBLE!

DOUBLE DOUBLE DOUBLE AND
TOIL AND TROUBLE BITCH   COME ON!
DOUBLE DOUBLE DOUBLE TOIL
AND TROUBLE!

(*rapping*)
DOUBLE DOUBLE DOUBLE AND TOIL
AND TROUBLE BITCH   OOOH!
   (DOUBLE DOUBLE TOIL AND TROUBLE)
DOUBLE DOUBLE DOUBLE TOIL AND TROUBLE!
   (BETTER GIT IT, BETTER GIT IT GIRL
ON THE DOUBLE)

DOUBLE DOUBLE DOUBLE AND TOIL
AND TROUBLE BITCH   COME ON!
   (DOUBLE DOUBLE TOIL AND TROUBLE)
DOUBLE DOUBLE DOUBLE BETTER
KILL THAT MOTHER!
   (BETTER GIT IT, BETTER GIT IT,
   YOU BETTER KILL THAT MOTHER)

Third Witch
DON'T LIKE HIS FACE

Second Witch
IT'S THE PRIVILEGE FOR ME.

First Witch
IT'S THE JUDGEMENT FOR ME

Woman
WELL WE BOUT TO SEE
HOW MUCH BLOOD

I. Lady Macbeth

WILL IT TAKE?
WILL IT TAKE . . . TO SET ME FREE?

Witches
DOUBLE DOUBLE TOIL AND TROUBLE
BETTER GIT IT BETTER GIT IT
GIRL ON THE DOUBLE!
DOUBLE DOUBLE TOIL AND TROUBLE—
DOUBLE DOUBLE TOIL AND TROUBLE!

> *The last note rings out a little too long as the* **Man** *takes the center-stage microphone. As he delivers the infamous Dagger speech, the* **Witches** *and* **Woman** *weave their voices around his.*

Man
Is this a dagger which I see before me,
The handle toward my hand? Come,
let me clutch thee:
I have thee not, and yet I see thee still.
Art thou not, fatal vision, sensible
To feeling as to sight? Or art thou but
A dagger of the mind, a false creation,   **Witches**
Proceeding from the heat-oppressed brain?   *Woah!*
Thou marshal'st me the way that I was going,
And such an instrument I was to use.
Mine eyes are made the fools o' th' other senses,
Or else worth all the rest. I see thee still;
And on thy blade and dudgeon gouts of blood,   **Witches**
Which was not so before. There's no such thing!   *mmm*
—I don't want this.
I don't want this!
Always reaching. Always wanting.
Asking me for more
Demanding more
Can't be more. I am what I am.
But I can't lose. Not to her
—Was told never lose

First Witch
Don't be too loose.

Man
Don't feel too much.

First Witch
Don't be violent, but be strong.

Man
Don't be a murderer but be prepared to kill.

First Witch
Be strong—

All Witches
Be strong!

Man
—it is the bloody business which informs
Thus to mine eyes.
Thou sure and firm-set earth,
Hear not my steps, which way they walk, for fear
The very stones prate of my whereabout,
Whiles I threat, he lives:
Words to the heat of deeds too cold breath gives.

> *A high-pitched note is played serving as a bell. It echoes and grows . . . as it grows, the tempo of the music accelerates.*

Man
I go, and it is done; the bell invites me.
Hear it not Duncan, for it is a knell
That summons thee to heaven, or to hell.

> *The **Band** launches into a drum and bass trip-hop remix of Double Double Toil and Trouble. The **Witches** arm the **Man**, rubbing his arms with blood and placing daggers in his hands.*

I. Lady Macbeth

Woman
GOT THAT BAD NEED
TO WIN AGAIN!
MAMA ALWAYS SAID
DON'T TRUST THESE MEN!

Witches
DON'T TRUST THESE MEN!
YEAH!

IF YOU NEED IT DONE
DO IT YOURSELF
EVEN IF IT MEANS
GOING STRAIGHT TO—

GOING STRAIGHT TO—

Man
(*halting music*)
I have done the deed.

Woman
Oh babe, that's great!

Man
Didst thou not hear a noise?

Woman
I heard the owl scream and the crickets cry.
Did not you speak?

Man
When?

Woman
Now.

Man
As I descended?

Woman
Ay.

Man
This is a sorry sight.

Woman
A foolish thought to say a sorry sight.

Man
Methought I heard a voice cry, "Sleep no more
Macbeth does murder sleep." The innocent sleep,
Sleep that knits up the ravell'd sleave of care,
The death of each day's life, sore labors bath.
Balm of hurt minds,
great nature's second course.
Chief nourisher in life's feast.

Woman
What do you mean?

Man
Still it cried, "Sleep no more" to all the house
"Glamis hath murder'd sleep, and therefore
Cawdor Shall sleep no more–
Macbeth shall sleep no more".

Woman
Who was it that thus cried?

> *The **Woman** climbs down from her singing position
> and gets closer to the **Man**.*

Woman
Why, worthy thane, you do unbend your noble
strength, to think
So brainsickly of things. Go get some water,
And wash this filthy witness from your hand . . .

> *The guitarist and bass player rattle through several tones.*

Woman
Why did you bring these daggers from the place?
They must lie there: go carry them; and smear the sleepy
grooms with blood.

Man

no no
  no no no.

Woman

Infirm of purpose!
Give me the daggers: the sleeping and the dead
Are but as pictures: 'tis the eye of childhood
That fears a painted devil. If he do bleed,
I'll gild the faces of the grooms withal; For it must seem their guilt.

> The **Band** *plays a series of rolling tones that fall to interrupting cacophonous sounds.*

Witches

TOIL AND TROUBLE
TOIL AND TROUBLE
TOIL AND TROUBLE
TOIL AND TROUBLE

Woman

My hands are of your colour; but I shame to
wear a heart so white.
I hear a knocking.
Hark! more knocking.
Get on your nightgown, lest occasion call us, and
show us to be watchers.
Be not lost so poorly in your thoughts.

Witches

DOUBLE DOUBLE TOIL AND TROUBLE!

> *With bloodied hands the* **Man** *and* **Woman** *run off stage. As soon as the two are out of sight the* **Witches** *drop their triumphant tableau.*
>
> *With their command work lights come up and all are able to find a moment of reprieve. The* **Band** *members take a well-deserved break. If they have waters or beers, or even*

a phone to check, now is a good time. However, even on break they remain interested in the scene as they too have been sucked into the story. A stage hand or two enter preparing for the next bit. A red carpet is rolled out, a chandelier brought in.

Pianist
Can we take a break?
That was a lot.

Second Witch
Yeah, you can take five.

*A **Witch** sits at the keys, and plays just enough to keep the space alive. Underscoring: Song 8 Coronation. Our **First Witch** steps forward addressing the audience. Like a soulful front woman she stirs up the crowd for our final portion of the show.*

First Witch	**Witches and Woman**
Women.	. . . yeah?
I said Women.	YEAH??

How you doing?
I mean for real. How are *we* doing?
Let's take a moment and figure it out.
Because ((clearly))) we need to figure it out.
Now . . .
I want you to think.
What is something that you want right now?
No really. Say it out loud.
Whisper it.
Breathe it.
Call it out.
It hasn't done us any good to sit on it
To wait for it
So it's time to speak it.
Because that's what this play is about too.
What's the worst that could happen? Really?

I. Lady Macbeth 63

You would speak something out loud, and someone might hear it.
That's it.
So what do you want?
For yourself?
In your life
Right now?
Do you need some time?
Do you need a check?
Touch?
Do you need some rest?
Do you need that glass half full again?

	Hallelujah!
What does it look like?	*Hallelujah!*
What would it feel like?	*Hallelujah!*
what's it going to take?	*Hallelujah!*

Beat.

And in the end	
Will it be worth it?	*Hallelujah!*

Woman
    (*re-entering*)
Girl.
It's worth it!
One, two, three, four!

> *Now as King and Queen,* **Woman** *and* **Man** *enter, processing through the space.*

Song 8: Hallelujah (Coronation)

Third Witch	**Woman**
IS HE GOOD TO YOU?	YEAH!
First Witch	
ARE YOU ON TOP, NOW?	YEAH!
Second Witch	
ARE YOU THE QUEEN NOW?	YEAH!

All
BENDED KNEES AND EVERYTHING . . .

Woman
OH YEAH YEAH!

Third Witch	**Woman**
IS HE GOOD TO YOU?	YEAH!

First Witch
ARE YOU ON TOP, NOW?

Second Witch
ARE YOU THE QUEEN NOW?   HELL YEAH!

Witches
TELL ME SIS, WAS IT WORTH IT!

Woman	**Witches**
WHAT'S UP EVERYONE	HALLELUJAH!
	HALLELUJAH!
IT'S YA GIRL AND I'M	HALLELUJAH!
BACK AT IT AGAIN.	HALLELUJAH!
GUESS WHAT . . .	
. . . I'M QUEEN NOW	HALLELUJAH!
	HALLELUJAH!

I SAID I'M QUEEN NOW . . .

> *The* **Woman** *signals to the* **Band** *and pulls us into a praise break; a joyous extended moment of song summoned by a pastor, preacher or spiritual leader meant to pull the audience somewhere deeper and acknowledge their need in the present.*

—NOW, MY SISTERS
I DON'T THINK THE PEOPLE HEARD ME
I SAID I'M WHAT?

Witches
QUEEN NOW!

I. Lady Macbeth 65

Woman
I SAID I'M THE WHAT?

Witches
QUEEN NOW!

Woman
AND THAT'S ALRIGHT!   **Witches**
EVERY DAY AND EVERY   ... EVERY DAY AND EVERY
NIGHT   NIGHT!
I SAID ... EVERY DAY AND   EVERY DAY AND EVERY
EVERY NIGHT   NIGHT
KING WHERE?   KING WHERE?
QUEEN NOW!   QUEEN NOW!
KING WHERE?   KING WHERE?
QUEEN NOW!   QUEEN NOW!

EVERY DAY AND EVERY   SHE'S THE QUEEN AND
NIGHT ...   THAT'S ALL RIGHT!
EVERY DAY AND EVERY NIGHT ...

> *The* **Woman** *pauses our praise break to find the* **Man**. *She holds a microphone to him.*

Man   **Witches**
... YOU'RE QUEEN.   SHE'S THE QUEEN AND
                            THAT'S ALRIGHT!

Woman   **Witches**
KING WHERE?   KING WHERE?
QUEEN NOW!   QUEEN NOW!
KING WHERE?   KING WHERE
QUEEN NOW!   QUEEN NOW!

Woman
I SAID IF YOU WOKE UP
AND LOOKED IN A. MIRROR AND SAW A QUEEN
THEN THAT'S ALL RIGHT!

Witches
ALL RIGHT!!!

The ensemble falls back into the story as the **Witches** *surround the* **Woman**.

First Witch
Well look at you.

Third Witch
—You look great!

Second Witch
Can we get down to business?

First Witch
Yeah.
Remember that lady in aisle three?
Her story?
our story?

Woman
Yes. Totally.

Second Witch
You got all this power
what you gonna do with it?

Woman
I'm gonna . . .
Question everything.

Witches
and?

Woman
Reclaim everything.

Witches
And?

Woman.
Buy my mother a house
—then I'm going to change the story
Change the system—

Second Witch
But you're queen now.
You are the system.
And . . . we're not done with her story.
Can't just skip around to the parts you like.

Woman
Okay.
What do I get to do?
What does Lady Macbeth get to do
after she's queen, after all of that?

Second Witch
You, get to host a dinner party.

Woman
. . . uh . . .

Second Witch
—and you get him.

Third Witch
You have to deal with him.

First Witch
So it's nice that you're already dressed. . . .

> *With this, the* **Witches** *leave the pair alone. In typical productions this a beat in which the Macbeths are alone in their home. Perhaps even a bedroom. A rare moment of intimacy. But this could take place in our initial rehearsal space vibe.*

Woman
How now? Why do you keep alone
Of sorriest fancies your companions making,
Using those thoughts which should indeed have died
With them they think on?
Things without remedy should be without regard
What's done is done.

Man
We have scorch'd the snake, not killed it.

Woman
  (*to audience*)
This is the turning point in the play.

Man
—She'll close and be herself; whilst our poor malice
Remains in danger of her former tooth.

Woman
Or rather
This is the less fun part in the play
for me.
for you, if you have to play *her*.
You don't get to do anything.

Man
—let the frame of things disjoint,

Woman
  (*to audience*)
These plays weren't written for women to actually perform.
They were written by a man for a bunch of other men to
play all of the roles.

Man
Ere we will eat our meal in fear, and sleep
In the affliction of these terrible dreams,
That shake us nightly. Better be with the dead.

I. Lady Macbeth   69

Woman
The jumps don't make sense
They are impossible to fill.

Man
No, they had a shared goal
They go for it.
they reach for it.
But who do they become?
And the most useful part of Shakespeare's rendering of this marriage
for me is . . .

Woman
—go on.

Man
Is that after they do the deed
They stop talking to each other.

Woman
Okay. What do we know.

Man
—we know that we love each other.

Woman
 . . . I guess.
It's hinted in the play
that they don't have children—

Man
There was one.
—we lost one.

Woman
Maybe from one line that I said earlier
Literally one line
You could *maybe* justify that they . . .

Man
—that we—

Woman
we lost a child.

Man
sure.

Woman
If a lady is unhappy it *must* be about a child.
If her character needs purpose
Make it about a baby. Somewhere somehow.
Someone's baby.
Make that her center
She simply cannot exist, without one.
It doesn't make sense.

Man
Your job is to make it make sense.

Woman
Okay I'll try. Let's try.

> *The musicians fall deeper into "I For You". Somehow, the space reflects the feeling of the song and what's between these two players. Everything flickers. The last dying flickers of warmth.*

Song 9: I For You

Woman
THIS IS THE PART THAT'S ALWAYS HARD
THEY'RE SO FAR APART.
I SHOULD BE CLOSE TO YOU

Man
She should you mean . . .

Woman
LOVE AND AMBITION WAS THE NAME OF THE GAME
NOW WE HAVE WHAT WE WANT

I. Lady Macbeth

Man
IN THE PLAY YOU MEAN . . .

Woman
YES, IN THE PLAY I MEAN.

Man
NOW THAT WE'RE KING AND QUEEN?

Woman
WHY DOES HE STOP LOVING SHE?
WHAT I NEED ISN'T WRITTEN IN THE SCENE
BUT CAN YOU GIVE?

Man
I CAN'T GIVE!

Woman
—GIVE MORE TO ME?

Man
I WON'T CRAWL ON ALL FOURS
I WON'T COME TO YOUR SIDE.
I CAN'T SEE IT YOUR WAY.

Both
THAT'S NOT THE WAY HE'S MADE.

Man
I MIGHT MAKE YOU SAD . . .

Woman
YOU MAKE ME MUCH MORE THAN THAT.
IT'S TOO HARD

> **Man**
> IN THE PLAY, YOU GET WHAT YOU GET

Man
IN THE PLAY
YOU GET WHAT
YOU GET . . .

Woman
IN THE PLAY
YOU GET WHAT YOU GET.

Woman
CAN IT BE I FOR YOU
THEN WE CAN SEE THIS THROUGH

Both
CAN IT BE I FOR YOU
THEN WE CAN SEE THIS THROUGH

Woman
CAN IT BE I FOR YOU
THEN WE CAN SEE THIS THROUGH

Both
IF IT'S I FOR YOU THEN WE CAN SEE THIS THROUGH
IF IT'S I FOR YOU THEN WE CAN SEE THIS THROUGH . . .

Man
I'LL ALWAYS BE RIGHT

Woman
I'LL ALWAYS BE YOURS

Man
I WON'T STAY ON MY SIDE

Woman
I'LL NEVER CRAWL ON ALL FOURS.

Man
I MIGHT MAKE YOU MAD . . .

Woman
YOU MAKE ME MUCH MORE THAN THAT
IT DOESN'T HAVE TO BE SO HARD . . .

Man
YOU KNOW YOU GET WHAT YOU . . .

Both
GET.

> *This musical moment ends, the two are close again,*
> *for a moment. A moment of peace between the two as*
> *collaborators and characters.*

Man / Woman
I—/ You . . .

Man
you go first.
It's your line first.

Woman
You must leave this.

Man
Full of scorpions is my mind dear wife.

Woman
Come on. Gentle my lord.
Sleek o'er your rugged looks.
Be bright and jovial among your guests tonight.

Man
Thou know'st that Banquo, and his son, lives.
There's comfort yet; they are assailable.
—be thou jocund.
There shall be done a deed of dreadful note.

Woman
What's to be done?

Man
Be innocent of the knowledge, dearest chuck—

> **Woman**
> Dearest chuck?

Man
—Till thou applaud the deed.

Woman
What do you mean?

Man
Come, seeing night—

> **Woman**
> Wait.

Man
Scarf up the tender eye of pitiful day;
And with thy bloody and invisible hand
Cancel and tear to pieces that great bond
Which keeps me pale.
Thou marvell'st at my words: but hold thee still—
Things bad begun make strong themselves by ill.

> *Before she can answer, the* **Witches** *return, bringing the banquet scene with them.* **Man** *joins the* **Band** *and* **Woman** *grabs the bottle of champagne, preparing a toast. The* **Witches** *enter the space, perhaps a bit more sparkly and done up as they are expecting a party and not having to suffer through marital strife.*

Woman
It's time right?

I. Lady Macbeth   75

First Witch
It is.

> **Third Witch**
> It's the banquet scene now.

Woman
Welcome to my castle.
You know what . . .
This is the Banquet scene everyone.
It's supposed to be a party.
So let's make a toast
Here's to us.
All of us.
Seriously thank you for coming out,
We really appreciate you, we do.
So cheers to everything we've been through.
And most of all, to the king.

> *Beat.*

—My lord you do not keep the cheer.
Say cheers!

Man
I'm good.

Woman
> (*recovering*)

How about a toast and a song—
Just sing that one from earlier
One, two three
In the place of . . .

> *The* **Witches** *pick up this impromptu moment of song, transforming "In the Place of Love" into an upbeat, brassy, Louisiana-style Second Line.*

Song 10: In the Place of Love (Reprise)

Woman / Third Witch
IN A PLACE OF LOVE . . .
LET'S CHEERS TO US!
MAY THERE ALWAYS BE GOOD TIMES Y'ALL

Woman, Witches
MAY THERE ALWAYS BE TRUST
IN A PLACE OF LOVE
LET'S TOAST TO US
MAY THE DARK DAYS
NEVER TOUCH US!
LORD LIFT ME—

Man
give me some wine!

Woman
—My noble lord

Song 11: Ghosts of Yesterday

Man
GIVE ME SOME WINE FILL FULL,
FILL FULL!

Man
IT USED TO BE WHEN MAN WAS SLAIN
DEAD THEY LAID.
LINE YOUR ENEMIES UP
NOTHING IN YOUR WAY

Woman
—NOT TODAY

Man
IT USED TO BE
A MAN COULD HAVE HIS SAY

I. Lady Macbeth 77

THE DAY WAS HIS
HE COULD HAVE HIS WAY

Woman, Witches
YOU DON'T GET TO ACT THIS WAY!

Man
I SEE THE DEAD
HEAR VOICES IN MY HEAD
MEN I KILLED, MEN SLAIN
BUT REALLY IT'S

Woman, Man, Witches
—THE GHOSTS OF YESTERDAY

Man
—THE THINGS OUR FATHERS SAY
ARE IN MY HEAD
IF I HAVE TO CHANGE
I'D RATHER BURN EVERYTHING!
THEY SAY—

Woman, Witches
—SLEEP NO MORE

Man
THEY SAY

Woman, Witches
—YOU'RE A FAKE

Man
THAT'S WHAT THEY SAY

Woman, Witches
—NO, DON'T LET ME DOWN

Man
 ... THEY SAY

Woman, Witches
YOU'RE A CLOWN!

Man
... THEY SAY

Woman
—CHANGE YOUR SKIN

Man
THAT'S WHAT THEY SAY.

Woman, Witches
—YOU'RE THE PROBLEM!

> *The* **Man** *holds centerstage—becoming a troubled rocker. His antics causing his body to thrust about the space. Our* **First Witch** *goes over to* **Woman** *offering her a reminder.*

First Witch
This is his mad scene, honey.
You don't have a say.
Me . . . you, everyone here
We're all just props for him to take up space.

Man
WHAT IF I'M SEEING THINGS?
AND I'M NOT OKAY?

Witches
NO ONE IS OKAY!

Woman
COUNTRIES BURN
FIRES RAGE!

Woman, Witches
EVERYTHING'S AT STAKE
IT'S NOT OKAY TO ACT THIS WAY!

Man
THEY SAY—

Witches
—SLEEP NO MORE

Man
THEY SAY

Witches
—HE'S A FAKE!

Man
THAT'S WHAT THEY SAY

Witches
—HE'LL LET YOU DOWN . . .

Man
 . . . THEY SAY

Woman
HE'S A CLOWN!

Man
 . . . THEY SAY

Witches
—CHANGE YOUR SKIN

| **Man** | **Witches** |
| THAT'S WHAT THEY SAY . . . | YOU'RE THE PROBLEM. |

80   All Is But Fantasy

*We hit the bridge of the song and it is a trippy, snake-like melody that winds, and winds. The **Man** is thrust further into Shakespeare's world.*

*Perhaps the **Witches** and the **Woman** become apparitions as well, moving to the music. We play with the double image of the **Man** becoming a minority in a group of Othered people, and Macbeth seeing ghostly apparitions in Shakespeare's Banquet Scene.*

Man
   (falling to Shakespeare)
Which of you have done this?
Can such things be,
You make me strange
Avaunt! And quit my sight!

Let the earth hide thee

Thy bones are marrowless.
Thy blood is cold
Hence, hence!

Witches

YOUR LEG CROOKED
CAUSE YOU FATHER LIED
YOU CRYING CAUSE YOUR
MAMA DIED
YOU NOT GOOD IN
CROWDS CUZ
IT'S IN THE BLOOD, IN
THE BLOOD
IN THE BLOOD
IN THE BLOOD!

First Witch
   (overlapping)
Eye of toad and all that shit
Twigs snapped and a little spit

Mama's smile and daddy's Black
A lil grease in the blood

   Third Witch/Woman
   (overlapping)

Second Witch
   (overlapping)
Scale of dragon, tooth of wolf
Witches' mummy, maw and gulf
Of the ravin'd salt-sea shark,

Root of hemlock digg'd i' the dark
Scale of dragon, tooth of wolf
Witches' mummy, maw and gulf

I. Lady Macbeth   81

    Your leg crooked cause you father lied
    You crying cause your mama died
    You not good in crowds cuz
    It's in the blood, it's in the blood

Witches
IT'S IN THE BLOOD, IT'S IN THE BLOOD
IN THE BLOOD, IN THE BLOOD!

Man
TAKE MY FACE, PEEL IT AWAY
TAKE THIS THREAD—RIGHT HERE
WHAT'S UNDERNEATH?
THERE'S NOTHING IT SEEMS

Woman
Sit, worthy friends. My lord is often thus
And hath been from his youth.
The fit is momentary,
If you much note him, you shall
Offend him and extend his passion:
Tis no other
Only it spoils the pleasure of time.
At once good night
Stand not upon the order of your going

But go at once.

> The **Band** *withdraws.*
> *Only the* **Man**, **Woman**, *and* **Witches** *remain.*
> *The* **Witches** *speak first . . .*

Second Witch
—LIL SISTA, WHY THE FROWN?

Third Witch
WORKED TOO HARD TO GET THAT CROWN.

First Witch
FIRE AND BRIMSTONE AND ALL THAT STUFF

Witches
SOMETIMES POWER IS NOT ENOUGH.

> *And then the **Witches** leave the **Woman** and **Man** alone to sort out what they can. If they can.*

Woman
Are you a man?

Man
Honestly . . .
I don't know what that is.

> *Beat.*

What would you have me be?

Woman
I wouldn't have you "be anything"
If it were up to me, you would // just be

Man
I'm playing the part.
Is the part the problem,
Or is it me?

Woman
It's not—

Man
Then play my part.

Woman
—no.

Man
You be Macbeth, I'll be the lady.

I. Lady Macbeth 83

Woman
I don't want to do that. I want to be the lady.

Man
Why? What do you want?
> *Beat.*
> *And then more time*

You just want to be the lead.

Woman
> *Beat.*

Maybe

Man
You're good.

Woman
Really? Thank you.
> *Beat.*

We have one more scene together in the play, so please . . .

Man
Yeah. Right.
—after the party.

Woman
After the party.
Your friends have left you.
War is coming
And you say—

Man
It will have blood; they say, blood will have blood.

Woman
> (*to audience*)

—and I think that's the moment she realizes

Things will never be the way she dreamed

Man
I am in blood stepped in so far, that should I wade no more—

Woman
He keeps saying I instead of we.

Man
—returning were as tedious as go'er.

> *He hands her his microphone, and leaves.*
> *a breath here.*

Woman
And I don't have much to say.
The scenes before the banquet and
this one after are the same.

> *A long beat here.*
> *She looks around noticing that she is the only player left.*
>
> *Relief for a moment.*
> *a look to the audience.*
>
> *and then the beginnings of something else.*

Woman
This is it, huh?
We're here already . . . ?
I ask myself every time we do this
Why does she go mad?

> *Beat.*

In the play, Shakespeare stays with her
only long enough to get the crown.
and then right when they should be closest
—When we should be thick as thieves He goes off
without her.
into action
into the world

I. Lady Macbeth   85

Full of purpose and plans
And she is, alone.
Maybe if it were easier in this world for a woman to go it alone.

> *She slips into talking to herself.*

What's the difference 'tween what you're told and what you know
What's the difference 'tween what you're told and what you—
I have something on my hand. It's from earlier.
Can you see that?
There's a spot. One second.
out damned spot!
Out, out, out, I say!

> *She turns away. Rubbing her hands. Breathing deeper.*
> *She falls to Shakespeare.*

—One, two. Why, then, 'tis time to do 't. Hell is murky!
Fie, my lord, fie! a soldier, and afeard?
What need we fear who knows it
When none can call our power to account?
The Thane of Fife had a wife
Where is she now
What, will these hands ne'er be clean?—
All the perfumes of Arabia
Will not sweeten this little hand
No, no, no, no
I'm rejecting this I can feel it.
I'm rejecting it.
I'm just . . . mad.
I'm so mad.
Do you know what I mean?
Why do they have to do this at the end?
Why do they write us this way?
Why do they imagine us this way?

> *Beat.*

I think they write us this way because they know.
They know what the world takes—what they take
They can't imagine living this way.

cabin'd, cribb'd, confined, I mean what am I wearing, bound in?

> *With this, she strips a part of her costume off. A corseted element that will remain a part of the storytelling.*

But this is the role, it's the one I always wanted.
The one I was taught to want.
Men get to run run around giving their best fucking Hamlet
Or any of the other hundreds of roles there are for
them to play
But if you happen to be a little too big, a little too small, or a little too black
You can't be the ingenue, you can't be this or that
so that leaves someone like Lady Macbeth
But that's okay because she's smart
and so that makes it contemporary.
she wants power, and so that makes it modern.
But at the end? But at the end of all that
Her death doesn't even happen onstage!
Her character is not centered in any way.
Her death doesn't have meaning
And I'm not—I . . .
I—

> *Instead of completing her thought with text the* **Woman** *finds her way back to the piano. She plunks a few notes summoning the final song of the evening. This can feel like she is writing in the moment or finding it.*

Song 12: Hallelujah (Finale)

Woman
I WALK, I REACH . . .
I THINK I BREATHE

I TRY I DANCE
I DIE I BLEED . . .

I THINK
    I WALK

I. Lady Macbeth

      I TRY . . . I LIVE
I LIVE, I LIVE, I LIVE
I . . . LIVE

Witches, Man
RAIN DOWN!

> *The* **Witches**, **Band** *and* **Man** *return helping her finish.*

Woman
I TRY AGAIN
I WORK I CLIMB

	Witches
I FIND I MAKE	CLIMB . . .
I FIND WHAT'S MINE!	
I BUILD HIM UP	OOH
AND TRY AGAIN	
I GIVE I GIVE I GIVE . . .	
I—	
EVERY TIME MY LOVER JUST WALKS BY	OOH
EVERY TIME THE WORLD SEEMS	OOH
TO ASK ME WHY	
EVERY TIME I'M DENIED . . .	DENIED
EVERY TIME YOU SEEM TO FIND A PLACE	OOH
EVERY TIME IT SEEMS, SEEMS SO SAFE	SAFE
EVERY TIME IT FALLS TO WASTE!	WASTE

YES I'M MAD.
YES I'M MAD.
AND I'M NO BETTER THAN THE LAST MAN
BUT I'LL TRY WHILE I LIVE
BEFORE I TURN TO—

<u>***An interruption.***</u>

First Witch
The queen, my lord, is dead.

Woman
Beat.

That was so fast.

Man
She should have died hereafter;

Woman
There was a whole other part I was going to do . . .

Man
There would have been a time for such a word.

Woman
. . . and it was going to be so good

Man	**Woman**
Tomorrow, and tomorrow, and tomorrow	Wait!

The percussionist keeps time in a steady 6/8 in the pocket as the following unfolds.

Woman
(spoken)
Wait

Witches.
Yes? / That's right. / Come on.

Woman
It's not going to go down this way.

First Witch
Then how's it going to go down?

Woman
Queen doesn't work.

Second Witch
That's right.

Woman
Queen, isn't real.

Third Witch
Correct.

Woman
So let's try again.
Not dead.

Man
Not dead?

Woman
Not queen.

Witches and Woman
Just woman.

All
Emilia.

Woman
Let's find her.

They tumble back into song, for one last round.

Woman	**Witches / Mad**
YES I'M MAD	YES I'M MAD

YES I'M MAD
AND I'M NO BETTER THAN THE LAST MAN
BUT I'LL TRY
WHILE I LIVE BEFORE I TURN TO
    DUST
    DUST
    DUST
    DUST

All

DUST	HALLELUJAH!		
DUST		HALLELUJAH!	
DUST			HALLELUJAH!
DUST!		HALLELUJAH!	
	HALLELUJAH!		
		HALLELUJAH!	
	HALLELUJAH!		
			HALLELUJAH!
		HALLELUJAH!	
			HALLELUJAH!
		HALLELUJAH!	

Woman
I THINK I WANT
IT'S NOT PROFOUND
IT MAKES ME MAD
IT TURNS ME ROUND

I THINK I WANT
AMBITION SAYS
TO LIVE, NOT DEAD
NOT DEAD, NOT DEAD . . .

> *Lights fall on our little group, our* **Band**, **Witches**, **Man**, **Woman** *and all as they lean in to what could be.*

II. Emilia

Before we can catch our breath and lights can settle the drummer starts a soulful clap-line. Our three **Witches**, *our guides and storytellers, join in first.*

Somehow, they have changed. They look much more like people you pass on the street. Dressed to move, dressed to work, dressed to enjoy the evening. But in shoes they could run in, if they had to.

They begin whispering, conjuring.

Witches
Once upon a time
Hail Mary full of grace
There was a black girl . . .

First Witch
It don't start that way.

Second and Third Witch
Then how does it go
What the Shakespeare man say?

First Witch
He say, all the little piggies ran home!

Second Witch
—to they wives!

Witches
Once upon a time
There was a play
Well a whole bunch of plays
Ended the same way

Rich lady, poor lady
Big and small
them ladies dead by Act Five
Yes, one and all
So . . .

Who are we?
who are you?
Do you even know
What's a lie, what's true?
If foul is fair
Then you're a witch too
And all the little piggies ran home

Third Witch
—tellin lies!

First Witch
Again!

Witches
Who are we?
We said, who are you!
What ya got to show
Your scars ain't cute!

This isn't a beginning and it isn't an end
This isn't a spell
And we're not friends

So cross your fingers
wiggle your toes
I bet you know the story
Of O-T-H-E-L-L-O

But do you know her?
How does hers go?
Say all your prayers
She gonna need them
Let's go!

II. Emilia

And then, we flip the switch. The **Women** *sing using bodies, hands, knees and anything needed to make rhythm and sound falling deeper into the blues which will be our musical idiom for the evening.*

Witches	**Third Witch**

Witches
HALLELUJAH
HALLELU!
HALLELUJAH
HALLELU!
HALLELUJAH
HALLELU

COME ON ...

THAT'S RIGHT!

SIT ON BACK AND CHECK THIS STORY
WE GOT TONIGHT!

HALLELUJAH
HALLELU!

Witches
HALLELUJAH
HALLELU
HALLELUJAH
HALLELU
HALLELUJAH
HALLELU!
HALLELUJAH
HALLELU!

TO BE A QUEEN
ISN'T WHAT IT SEEMS
POOR THING ...
POOR THING!

THESE ARE THE STORIES
WE KNOW HOW IT GOES
FROM TOP TO END
BUT I'M NOT DEAD!

Witches
—NOT DEAD, NOT DEAD
NOT DEAD, NOT DEAD
NOT DEAD, NOT DEAD
NOT DEAD, NOT DEAD   ONE MORE TIME!

NOT DEAD NOT DEAD
NOT DEAD NOT DEAD

All Is But Fantasy

NOT DEAD NOT DEAD
NOT DEAD NOT DEAD

OH LET'S . . .
TRY ANOTHER WAY
TAKE ME ROUND ONE
MORE TIME

Woman
—Not doing that again.
The queen thing?
Over it.
Lady Macbeth?
A slogan.
I'm just a regular—shmegular girl
At my job.
At my home
Waiting for my turn
And you know what?
I got nothing to prove.
Better that way.
The crown?
Whatever.
The throne?
What's that?
It's not real.
What's real is . . .
The bills.

All Witches
Okay?

Woman
The price of food.

All
That's right.

First Witch
Working six days a week

Third Witch
—seven

Woman
Just to get by.
What's real is—

Third Witch
the working class

Second Witch
the folks who think they are working class

First Witch
but never have been and never will be

Woman
You know,
us folks
with our heads down.

First Witch
Backs against the wall.

Woman
The people who clean your homes

Second Witch
—and fry your chips

Third Witch
Fighting in the wars of yesterday and tomorrow.

Woman
They want things.

All
We want things.

Woman
And so I want things.
But the whole . . .
> (*falling into Lady Macbeth*)

All Women
unsex me here . . . ?

Woman
Kill the king and get on top?
that didn't work.
So . . . let's try something different.
something simpler.
Let's try

Woman and Witches
Emilia.

Woman
But let's keep with the rock and the blues and the rock.
Mostly blues though.
Because for me, Emilia's song is a blues song.

Witches
> (*singing*)

HALLELUJAH
HALLELU!

> *During this next sequence a* **Witch** *hands the* **Woman** *a makeup-remover wipe. She wipes off every inch of makeup she had on.*

Woman
Emilia.
Remember her?
She doesn't have her own play
She is all the way tucked away
Up and in

First Witch
—inside the one with the big O—

Witches
(*making an arpeggiated chord*)
O
    O
                O
                        O

Witches
Othello!

Woman
I'm sure we remember that one.
    (*to the* **Witches**)
Set me up.

> *The* **Witches** *build a polyrhythm. A pyramid of sound being made right in front of our eyes. The bassist and guitarist build on this rhythm with knocking and clicking sounds.*

Witches
Emilia!

First Witch
Iago's wife.

Second Witch
The villain's wife.

Third Witch
—Don't give it away!

First Witch
I'm not giving anything away.
This story is old.

Third Witch
the other woman in the play.

First Witch
Emilia is the one who often gets her stuff cut.

Woman
Her lines and scenes and little bits.

Third Witch
At least Emilia has faith!

Second Witch
why else would she stay?

Woman
I think she has to have faith.

First Witch
In what, her man?

Man
Iago.

Woman
I'm sure you've heard of him.

> *The* **Man** *steps out of shadow and begins to embody Iago. He picks up his guitar, and plays that for the evening.*
>
> *We fall into our second blues number. A soulful, creeping, and strong blues song reminiscent of Howling Wolf. The* **Band** *is sweating before we even begin.*

Song 2: Roll the Dice

Man
THIS TIME AROUND, JUST ROLL THE DICE.
IT ALL ENDS JUST THE SAME, BUT JUST TRY.

I'M A MAN WHO FEELS ENTITLED
IT'S A STORY AS OLD AS TIME

I DON'T KNOW WHY I LIKE WHAT I LIKE
IT'S IN MY DNA, HARD AS I TRY!
JUST A MAN WHO FEELS ENTITLED!
KICK ME DOWN, 'GONE AHEAD AND TRY!

Woman
MEN WANT WHAT THEY WANT, WHAT THEY WANT
SOME WILL LIE FOR WHAT THEY WANT, WHAT THEY WANT
TURN A BLIND EYE 'CAUSE YOU'RE IN LOVE
BUT THAT EYE CAN'T STAY BLIND FOR LONG

Witches
THAT EYE CAN'T STAY BLIND FOR LONG

> *The* **Band** *dips down, underscoring the following over the verse pattern.*

Woman
What happens when a woman picks the wrong one?

Man
I hate the Moor.
And it is thought abroad, that 'twixt my sheets
He has done my office.

Woman
Their jealousy isn't so bad at first.

Man
I know not if 't be true—

Woman
They hate the world but love you!
and that makes you special.

A moment of physicality between the two that is initiated by the **Man**.

Woman
Now, Iago may be many things
but you can't deny that he's focused.

Man
The Moor is of a free and open nature,
That thinks men honest that but seem to be so
and will as tenderly be led by the nose
As asses are.

Woman
He's not riding around the Scottish bog
shitting his pants in the middle of the night
over a little blood.
He wants to do something, he does it.
He has a bit of a wandering eye—

Man
Now, I do love her too—
Not out of absolute lust
But partly led to diet my revenge—
For that I do suspect the lusty Moor
Hath leap'd into my seat.
the thought whereof
Doth, like a poisonous mineral, gnaw my inwards;
And nothing can or shall content my soul
Till I am even'd with him, wife for wife.
  (*cueing the* **Band**)

Let's go!

A breath as the **Woman** *realizes that she is not the only band leader for the evening.*

Man
LISTEN, THIS TIME I'M NOT PLAYING NICE
IN THIS LIFE, NO CRIME IS A CRIME.

CAN'T A MAN HAVE MORE IN HIS LIFE?
BY ANY MEANS, I GOTTA GET MINE.

Woman
MEN WANT WHAT THEY WANT, WHAT THEY WANT
SOME WILL LIE FOR WHAT THEY WANT, WHAT
THEY WANT
YOU TURN A BLIND EYE BECAUSE YOU'RE
IN LOVE
BUT THAT EYE CAN'T STAY BLIND FOR LONG

Witches and Woman
MEN WANT WHAT THEY WANT, WHAT THEY WANT
SOME WILL LIE FOR WHAT THEY WANT, WHAT
THEY WANT
YOU TURN A BLIND EYE BECAUSE YOU'RE IN LOVE
BUT THAT EYE CAN'T STAY BLIND FOR LONG.

THAT EYE CAN'T STAY BLIND FOR LONG.

> *We push to a tense, soulful underscore. Lights focus on our same* **Man** *who is now near our* **Band**. *He is much more comfortable with them now. He speaks to them, the audience his god if he has one, and his guitar.*

Man
When devils will the blackest sins put on
They do suggest at first with heavenly shows,
As I do now for whiles this honest fool
Plies Desdemona to repair his fortunes
And she for him pleads strongly to the Moor,
I'll pour this pestilence into his ear,
That she repeals him for her body's lust;
And by how much she strives to do him good,
She shall undo her credit with the Moor.
So will I turn her virtue into pitch,
And out of her own goodness make the net
That shall enmesh them all.

Woman
MEN WANT WHAT THEY WANT, WHAT THEY WANT
SOME WILL LIE FOR WHAT THEY WANT, WHAT
THEY WANT
I TURN A BLIND EYE BECAUSE I'M IN LOVE
BUT THAT EYE CAN'T STAY BLIND FOR LONG

Witches
MY EYE CAN'T STAY BLIND FOR . . .

Man and Woman
MY EYE CANT STAY BLIND . . .

All
FOR LONG

> *And then the nastiest, heavy guitar line finishes this one out for us. We shift, focusing on the* **Woman** *and* **Witches**. *From jump,* **Third Witch** *has an issue. She makes it clear.*

First Witch
Can we . . .
Can we just have a check in?

Woman
What's the problem?

Third Witch
Are we really doing this one?

Woman
Yes. Why not?

Third Witch
But *this* one . . .
This play

It's not cute.
It's a bit mad actually?

Woman
Emilia is one of us.
    (*to audience*)
Someone like me.

First Witch
A person of other.

Woman
Because Desdemona has the whole
fragility thing down.
    (*to audience*)
It's true.
She is that.
She is the definition.
She is the reason.

Third Witch
If she is the reason
Then you're going to need help that we can't give you.

> *The* **Witches** *conjure a new player: our* **Desdemona**
> *for the evening. She enters the space perhaps with an
> instrument. She fits with the other women in every way,
> another lead singer for the* **Band**.
>
> *Underscoring shifts to a pre-rise of "Straight Line".*

Third Witch
You're going to need her.
You're going to need . . .

Desdemona and All
(with power)
Desdemona.

Woman
Tell me about her.

Second Witch
it girl.

First Witch
—rich girl.

Desdemona
good school.

Third Witch
New money.

Desdemona
The *ingenue*.

Second Witch
A symbol.

First Witch
A "white ewe".

Man
"Gentle Desdemona"

Desdemona
—They call me.

Man
a land carrack and lawful prize.

Desdemona
a land carrack.
a rich merchant ship.
a prize because of money.
because of beauty

Second Witch
A prize because of whiteness.
Is that too far a leap?

Man
—"a maid
That paragons description and wild fame."

Desdemona
A "most exquisite lady" . . .

Third Witch
"the grace of heaven"

First Witch
"Full of the most blessèd condition"

Man
"Sport for Jove".
A "delicate creature"
—an inviting eye

Second Witch
A modest eye.

Desdemona
   (*insisting*)
—a fine woman.
fair woman.
sweet woman.
I feed well.

love company
Am free of speech
I sing, I play. I dance well
I am all but a fantasy.

First Witch
—and she has skin

Man
whiter than snow.

>*Beat.*

She is indeed perfection.

Third Witch
So . . . you?

Woman
me?

Witches
we.

All
Us.

First Witch
—being *other*

All
being Emilia

Second Witch
Are here. In this play
Compared to this woman . . .

Witches and Woman
who is—

Man
Perfection.

Woman
and I'm supposed to be married to this person?
That's not a good feeling.
Not only sidekick but
But just
The other woman?

Desdemona
I think these characters
These women are actually
They are close to each other. What?
That's what I think. They *can* be close to each other.
Just two wives caught in-between, you know?
Equal ground.

Woman
So in the play
You and Othello are—

Desdemona
   (*falling to Shakespeare, to audience*)
That I did love the Moor to live with him,
My downright violence and storm of fortunes
May trumpet to the world: my heart's subdued
Even to the very quality of my lord.
I saw Othello's visage in his mind,
And to his honour and his valiant parts
Did I my soul and fortunes consecrate.

First Witch
Look at that.

Second Witch
Rich folks never do things like the rest of us.

Third Witch
She's not just in love, it's EPIC
EARTH-SHATTERING love.

First Witch
Loud love.

Second Witch
Out in the open

First Witch
For everyone to see.

Woman
So.
She falls in love with someone she's not supposed to.
A man

Man
My friend.

Woman
Your very *best* friend.
But let's not make it all about him.

Man
Above me in rank.
In title.
In stature.

Woman
—and to get ahead . . .

Man
He, Othello, moves someone *else* above me, instead.

Woman
And then I
My character is—

II. Emilia

*Underscoring kicks in. Drums propel us forward. 4/4 as the cast is thrust into Shakespeare's scene. The **Women** comment on the action, and the **Man** plays the scene out.*

Man
   (*to a **Band** member*)
Call up her father—
What ho, Brabantio!

Woman
Middle of the night.

Man
Zounds, sir, you're robbed.
Even now, now, very now, an old black ram
Is tupping your white ewe!

Second Witch
Black sin.

First Witch
Black ram.

Third Witch
Whatever works.

Man
I am one, sir, that comes to tell you your daughter
and the Moor are now making the beast with two backs.

Woman
. . . and then I'm dragged to some underground trial—

First Witch
   (*as **Desdemona**'s father*)
The Duke in council?
In this time of the night? Bring him away;
Mine's not an idle cause.

Woman
Where she is—

Desdemona and Women
Disowned.

Second Witch
Her father says . . .

Third Witch
    (*as Brabantio*)
God be with you! I have done.
Please it your Grace, on to state affairs.

Woman
State affairs?

All
    war.

Woman
Always.

Second Witch
    (*as a man of state*)
The Turk with a most mighty preparation makes for Cyprus.

Woman
Cyprus?

Desdemona
Dear lords, if I be left behind,
A moth of peace, and he go to the war
The rites for why I love him are bereft me
Let me go with him.

Third Witch
(*as a man of state*)
Honest Iago,
My Desdemona must I leave to thee.
I prithee let thy wife attend on her.

Second Witch
You must away tonight.

> *A breath. Underscoring shifts to an indie blues feel the* **Witches**, **Woman** *and* **Man** *prepare for what is next.*

Woman
I Emilia am a wordless character only referred to as—

Desdemona
A wife.

Woman
And it is said to me that I will—

Desdemona
Attend on me.

Woman
Attend meaning wait upon.
Attend meaning serve
—Serve meaning

Desdemona
But it doesn't have to be that way.
we don't have to—

Woman
There are two things that are clear.
That I'm married to him
and I don't order people around

I *get* ordered around
So does my husband.
But you want to be friends?

Desdemona
Of course.

Woman
I understand.
I do it too.
I go to the salon
Ask the manicurist her name

Third Witch
—ask her if she has kids

Woman
—how she's doing

First Witch
. . . laugh

Third Witch
—and play nice
And pretend
As someone haunches over
my city feet
Filing and scraping
fast as they can
For a wage.

Desdemona
Being friends will make it easier.

Woman
    Beat.
If I *don't* want to be your friend
Then what happens?

Desdemona
Then I think you'll be *very* lonely at the end.
At the end of this play.

Woman
. . . Right.

Desdemona
All we have is each other.

Woman
In this play, that certainly is true.
Is it really possible to be friends?

>   *Beat.*

—when we were children
it was easier

First Witch
To extend a hand.

Second Witch
To see no difference.

Woman
But with time . . .

All Witches
It gets harder.

Woman
Because with *time*
ring around the rosie

Witches
and . . .

Desdemona
—do you want to sleepover my house?

Woman
Turns into

Third Witch
You cutting me in line.

First Witch
Telling me to move out of your way.

Second Witch
Looking at me twice if I'm promoted over you

First Witch
Or if I dare to have an inch of what you have.

Desdemona
And what about the big A?

Woman
Ambition?

Desdemona
No, allyship.

Woman
That's even worse.

Desdemona
    (*to the* **Witches**)
Can you help us please?

First Witch
    (*to both women*)
Look.
There are no witches in this play.
Macbeth had the spirits
But you . . . Both of you?
There's no one pulling your strings.

There's no god
only men.

Woman
Then why are you here?

First Witch
Sweetie, we're here for the music.
    (*gesturing to audience*)
and we're here for them.
Remember that.

Desdemona
One, two, three, four

Song 3: Straight Line

Desdemona
WHAT YOU WERE TOLD
'S WHAT YOU BELIEVE . . . AND
THE ENDING COULD BE SO
DIFFERENT FOR YOU AND ME

WHY CAN'T YOU SEE?
WHY CAN'T YOU DREAM?
YOU'RE STANDING THERE IN THE WATER
IT'S GETTING DEEP

Witches
OOOH
ITS GETTING DEEP

Woman
Listen . . .

Desdemona
—I GET IT BABE
HISTORY SPEAKS, AND
THE LINE IS LONG BETWEEN

Witches
THEN AND NOW
AND YOU AND ME

Desdemona
FRIEND'S A WORD
THESE WOMEN NEED
AROUND THE CLASS LINES
BY ANY MEANS

Woman
—Wait

Desdemona	**Woman**
YOU WANNA GIVE ME	I MIGHT GIVE YOU A
A HARD TIME?	HARD TIME
YOU WANNA MAKE	I MIGHT MAKE THE
THE ASSUMPTION?	ASSUMPTION

BUT I BELONG HERE NEXT TO YOU
PLEASE DON'T SING ABOUT A MAN
BECAUSE THAT'S NOT THAT DEEP YOU SEE
BUT OUR MELODY . . . COULD BE
SWEET.

SO TELL ME YOUR STORY
SHOW ME WHAT YOU SEE
BECAUSE THE PAGES IN BETWEEN
ARE BLANK FOR YOU AND ME

I DARE YOU TO GET DEEP
I DARE YOU TO TRUST THE MELODY

Desdemona
   (*spoken*)
Tell me your story.
Not hers, but yours.

Woman
Okay.
I'D BE YOUR FRIEND

IF YOU COULD SEE THAT WHEN IT SERVES
YOU STEP IN FRONT
AND OVER ME

YOU'LL SAY MOVE ASIDE
"LET ME SPEAK"
YOU THINK WE'RE THE SAME?
THAT'S A LIE IF YOU ASK ME

YOU WANNA HOLD HANDS?
WALK SIDE BY SIDE DOWN THE STREET
WELL IT'S HARD TO BUY IN

AND I CAN'T HIDE THE FACT
THAT I'D BE BETRAYING PART OF ME
YET, I AGREE
OUR MELODY IT COULD BE
SWEET . . .

Desdemona
SO TELL ME YOUR STORY
SHOW ME WHAT YOU SEE
BECAUSE THE PAGES IN BETWEEN
ARE BLANK FOR YOU AND ME

SO TELL ME YOUR STORY
SHOW ME WHAT YOU SEE
BECAUSE THE PAGES IN BETWEEN
ARE BLANK FOR YOU AND ME

I DARE YOU TO LET IT GET DEEP
I DARE YOU TO TRUST THE MELODY
I DARE YOU TO SEE ME . . .

> *The music finishes here. Lights pull to our two women and we focus on them. They try again.*

Desdemona
Friend?

Woman
For now.

> *Shift.*

So what did you do?
What does your *character* do?

Desdemona
My character falls in love.
That's it. That is her crime.

Woman
Mine too.

First Witch
And? So what?
What's so hard to understand about that?
What is so hard to understand about a woman . . .

Third Witch
—a wife

First Witch
A wife who gets dragged into her husband's story?

Second Witch
Pick a headline. Watch the news.

Third Witch
It is how the story *can* go.

Woman
—but

First Witch
But what?

Woman
Emilia is such an afterthought.
It kills me.

Desdemona
No. The play is gonna kill you.
So we shouldn't waste the precious time we have *together*
going over what makes us different
or what makes this hard.
What's more important is that our lovely, devoted husbands are soldiers.
Soldiers who are friends.
—and these friends, these soldiers are killers.

    Beat.

So yeah. We're an afterthought sweetie.
To their pain
Their brotherlyyyyy pain.

Woman
In the play what draws you to him?
—what draws Desdemona to Othello?

Desdemona
He speaks so well.

Woman
Ugh.

Desdemona
What?

First Witch
Nothing, that's just a thing

Second Witch
Like Obama. . . .?

Desdemona
That's not // what I meant.

Woman
It's a kind of cringe thing that—

Desdemona
No, no.
I'm not trying to be cringe.

Third Witch
That's what people say
To make *us* stand out from each other

Woman
I think this is where that very trope begins.

Second Witch
That a Black man who speaks well
is different than the rest of us.
anyways
Go on.

Desdemona
What draws you to him?
What draws Emilia to Iago?

Woman
I . . . I don't know.
We're just, together. That's just how it is in the play.
    (*to audience*)
Isn't that how it works?

Desdemona
I had an ex whose sister was dating such a man.

Woman
—What do you mean by . . .

Desdemona
A man who wore a uniform.
A man who could be considered an Iago

Second Witch
Why didn't she leave?

Desdemona
I don't know.
But her sadness was sort of . . . just all over her.
    (*to audience*)
—Wait. Before people get offended
Half my family is in the military or has been in the military
at some point in their lives.
So I'm not coming from a place of judgement
I love my family and respect their choice.
But being in the military can do different things to different
people.

Third Witch
—yeah but the woman?

Desdemona
so my ex's sister
she said to me

Woman
Where were you guys?

Desdemona
We took her kids and went to a
Like beer—relay at the local
super-mom's house.

Woman
A beer relay?

Desdemona
Yeah.
People could bring their kids
And the kids and adults would run a kilometer
and after each quarter you chug a beer

—if you're an adult.
If you're a child then you just run.
Anyways this woman
she said to me—

Third Witch
(as a housewife)
"Love may not look the way you want it to.
But love is love."

Woman
Love is love?

Desdemona
That's what she said.

Woman
Beat.
how many times I've heard
out of the mouths of women I love—

Desdemona
"men will be men"

First Witch
"Men do what they do"

Second Witch
"That's just how it is"

Third Witch
"there's nothing you *can* do"

Desdemona
"They can't be all good"

Woman
Why do smart women choose these men?

Desdemona
How do we know our characters are smart?

Woman
Their words.

Desdemona
—Actions speak louder than words.

Woman
>(*to* **Man**)

Come here.

> *Underscore shifts to a blues-rock song that is reminiscent of "Lookin' Good" by Magic Sam. This one should roll and roll, leaving the audience wishing it never ended.*
>
> *Underscoring begins.*

Woman
>(*to* **Man**)

Tell me a joke.

Man
Okay.
>*Beat.*

What's the difference between a blonde and an ironing board?

Woman
What.

Man
An ironing board's legs are hard to open.

First Witch
Okay.
Tell her another.

Man
What's the difference between a blonde and a mosquito?

Woman
I dunno. What?

Man
A mosquito stops sucking when you slap it.
What's the difference between a blonde and peanut butter?
Nothing.
Neither of 'em care if you stick it in them.

Desdemona
Okay, enough.

Man
What does a blonde say after sex?

Woman
She said, enough.

Man
What's the best thing about dating a Black girl?

Desdemona
... I don't think we should ...

Woman
It's fine.
Let him go for it.

Man
You don't have to meet her father.

> *Beat.*
> (*without stopping*)

How does a Black girl tell if she is pregnant?
When she pulls the tampon out all the cotton is picked.

Woman
Okay. Stop.

Man
Isn't that what you want?

Woman
Not really.

Man
You want me to be as bad as I can be?

Woman
No I just need you to be Iago.

Desdemona
Same thing.

Man
Can you take a break?

Woman
It's okay.

> **Desdemona** *and our* **Witches** *do so, but they don't stray too far. One* **Woman** *leaves, another leaves and peers through the window, another exits into the house.*

Man
What do you want?
You want to cut past all the nuance
and brilliance of this play
Of the offering that is this character
—my character—
And zero in on the bad?

I'm not saying I disagree with you.
I know there are plenty of problems in this play.

Woman
This isn't about "problems".
—This is about the guts.
The insides of these characters
and what it takes to play them.
What it costs.

Man
Please don't lecture me.

Woman
How many productions have we seen with a handsome charismatic Iago
who gets to do whatever he wants?
Whenever people want to do Othello,
You're the obsession.

Man
You think I'm handsome and charismatic?
Iago *is* charismatic
That's part of the good and part of the bad.
Come here.

Woman
I don't even like you.

Man
Yes you do.

> *The* **Man** *makes an attempt to soften her and lightly counts us into the next ear worm . . .*
>
> *This should be disorienting and darkly romantic.*
>
> *The pair dance a dark, pedestrian tango. Their legs move to the rhythm in a hypnotic, strange way.*

Song 4: Be Not Acknown of It

Man
I CAN PLAY NICE
BUT IT'D BE A BORE
I THINK YOU PREFER
SOMEONE MORE S U R E

SOMEONE WITH TEETH
SOMEONE LIKE ME
I'LL EAT THE WORLD
STAND BESIDE ME

	Witches
WE ARE SO SMALL	BA BA BA BA BA BA BA BA
THAT'S WHAT THEY SAY	BA BA BA DA
BUT . . . IT ISN'T TRUE	BA BA BA
	BA BA BA DA

Woman
THEY . . . JUST LIKE IT THAT WAY
THEY . . . KEEP US LOW
WHY CAN'T WE HAVE MORE?

Woman
IT'S NOT ABOUT COLOR

Both
I JUST WON'T DIE SORE!

Woman
I KNOW YOU, YOU
AND YOU KNOW ME
I KNOW YOU, YOU
AND YOU KNOW ME

Man
MY HEART IS BLACK

Woman
BLACK, BLACK JUST LIKE LIKE ME

Man
LET'S EAT THE RICH!

Woman
THROW THEM IN A PIT, LET'S SEE
WE'RE UNDERFOOT

Man
WE'RE UNDER THEIR BOOT

Woman
LET'S GET WHAT WE CAN

Man
JUST ME AND YOU

Women
I KNOW YOU, YOU
AND YOU KNOW ME
I KNOW YOU, YOU
AND YOU KNOW ME

Women
I KNOW YOU, YOU
AND YOU KNOW ME
I KNOW YOU, YOU
AND YOU KNOW ME

> *At the end of this our women have returned with flowers, drinks and more toys on hand.* **Desdemona** *interrupts the pair. She cues a heavy funk number. A callback to Suge Otis and James Brown. However she interrupts, let's give her a loudspeaker and let her talk her shit.*

Desdemona
Excuse me.
Sorry to interrupt but . . .

Song 5: Two Cents

Desdemona
WHY'D YA FALL IN LOVE?
SAID WHY'D YA FALL IN LOVE?
IT DON'T MAKE NO
NEVA DID, NEVA WILL, NO
NEVER EVER, GONNA MAKE NO SENSE!
LOVIN' MEN

Woman, Desdemona and Witches
IT'S IRRATIONAL!
IRRESPONSIBLE!
IRREPLACEABLE!
PURELY SENSATIONAL!
IT WON'T MAKE NO, CAN'T MAKE NO
NEVER EVER . . . EVER GONNA MAKE NO SENSE!
LOVIN' MEN

Desdemona
WHY'D YA FALL IN LOVE?
SAID WHY YA FALL IN LOVE?

Woman and Desdemona
IT WASN'T FOR NO VIRGIN MARY,
OH HAIL MARY!
GOOD INTENTIONS, HE HE NEVER HAD

Woman
BUT D'YOU KNOW WHAT?
I SAID DO YOU KNOW . . .
WE DO IT WITH THE LIGHTS ON!

Woman, Desdemona
WE D, D, DO IT WITH THE LIGHTS ON!

Desdemona and Witches
IT'S IRRATIONAL!
IRRESPONSIBLE!
IRREPLACEABLE!
PURELY SENSATIONAL!
IT WON'T MAKE NO, CAN'T MAKE NO
NEVER EVER ... EVER GONNA MAKE NO
SENSE!
LOVIN' MEN

Desdemona	**Witches**
NOW,	
MAMA SHE ALWAYS SAID	WHAT SHE SAY, WHAT SHE SAY?

SHE SAY KEEP YA TWO CENTS
IF IT AIN'T FOR THE BILL
AND ACT LIKE YA GOT SOME SENSE!

First Witch
BUT WITH HIM YOU WEREN'T THINKING
NOT WITH YOUR HEAD

Woman and Desdemona
I WAS THINKIN' BOUT THE MARRIAGE BED!

Witches
I WAS THINKIN' BOUT THE MARRIAGE BED

All
IT'S IRRATIONAL!
IRRESPONSIBLE!
IRREPLACEABLE!
PURELY SENSATIONAL!
IT WON'T MAKE NO, CAN'T MAKE NO
NEVER EVER ... EVER GONNA MAKE NO
SENSE!
YOUR LOVE FOR MEN

Desdemona, Woman
BUT, OOH WE PRAY
OOOH WE HOPE
WE HOPE IT ALL ENDS WELL
OOH WE HOPE OUR DEVOTION
WILL HAVE MEANING
FOR THEY ARE THE ONLY ONE.

Woman, Desdemona, Witches
FOR THEY ARE THE ONLY ONE.
FOR THEY ARE THE ONLY ONE!
... OR SOMETHING LIKE THAT! (BARF)

Desdemona
Come on then.
Back to the play.
To Cyprus.

Woman
To Cyprus.

> **Desdemona** *draws near the center of our cramped playing space, finding a bucket that has been used for cigarettes during the piece. She and the* **Witches** *dump its contents out in the middle of the room leaving a pile of sand, stubs and ash.*
>
> *With a cue from the* **First Witch** *the percussionist begins a Vaudevillian drum roll. As he does, the* **Man** *steps forward again, near the pile.*

Third Witch
Innnnnnnnnnnnnnntroducccccccing
The man.
The monster.
The snake of Cyprus.
your male lead and star ...
The one we keep returning to again and again ...
Iago.

*The **Man** grabs a microphone and stands somewhere a little too close to the audience. A little too high. He is trouble. He steals someone's drink and makes an announcement.*

All are a tad too inebriated. Perhaps someone moons the audience, another spills something. Stifled laughs and all are too loose.

Man
It is Othello's <u>P L E A S U R E</u>, our noble and valiant general, that importing the mere perdition of the Turkish fleet,
every man put himself into triumph.
some to dance, some to make bonfires,
each man to what sport and revels *his addiction* leads him. For besides these beneficial news, it is the celebration of his nuptial.
All offices are open, and there is full liberty of feasting from this **present** hour of five
till the bell have told eleven.
Heaven bless the isle of Cyprus and our noble general, Othello.

Song 6: Oh Brother

Man
    (*singing*)
BROTHER OH BROTHER
NOTHING ELSE TO BE . . .

BROTHER OH BROTHER
NOTHING ELSE TO DO

CAN'T BE SORRY
CAN'T BE BLUE
BECAUSE THE SUN SHINES ON ALL OF US!

II. Emilia

Now, I
TOOK MY DEMON FOR A WALK
WE SPENT SOME TIME, WE HAD A TALK
TO MY DISMAY
HE MADE SENSE

I CAN DO MY WORK
LIGHTS ON OR OFF
WALK THE LINE
AND TALK THE TALK
DOESN'T SEEM TO MATTER
NO, NOT AT ALL
BECAUSE . . . THE SUN SHINES ON ALL OF US

Man	**First Witch**
RICH MAN POOR MAN	HEY
AIN'T THE SAME	NO, WE AIN'T THE SAME
WE'RE NOT LIVING, WE AIN'T DYIN'	WE AIN'T LIVIN THE SAME WAY
THE SAME WAY	

I CAN DO MY WORK
LIGHTS ON OR OFF
I CAN WALK THE LINE
AND TALK THE TALK
BUT IT DOESN'T SEEM TO MATTER
NO, NOT AT ALL
BECAUSE . . . THE SUN IT SHINES ON ALL OF US

All
THE SUN IT SHINES ON ALL OF US
THE SUN IT SHINES ON ALL OF US
THE SUN IT SHINES ON ALL OF US
THE SUN IT SHINES ON ALL OF US

Man	**Women**
LOOK IN THE BARREL	I LOOK, I REACH, I WALK
WHAT DO YOU SEE?	

Man
SITTIN AT THE BOTTOM IS
YOU AND ME
YOU AND ME
DROP IN A BUCKET THAT'S
WHAT THEY SAY
NONE OF US WILL MAKE IT OUT TODAY

Women
IT'S YOU AND ME!

A DROP, A DROP

Man
LOOK IN THE BARREL
WHAT DO YOU SEE?
SITTIN AT THE BOTTOM IS YOU AND ME
YOU AND ME

All
THE SUN IT SHINES ON ALL OF US
THE SUN IT SHINES ON ALL OF US
THE SUN IT SHINES ON ALL OF US
THE SUN IT SHINES ON ALL OF US

THE SUN IT SHINES ON ALL OF US
THE SUN IT SHINES ON ALL OF US
THE SUN IT SHINES ON ALL OF US
THE SUN IT SHINES ON ALL OF US

As the music warps the players move faster.

Woman
Something is wrong.
I think upon it. I smell it.

All
Villainy.

An accent from the percussionist.

Woman
That's how it is in the story.
In the play.

Can't quite put my finger on it.
After this party my character only has ins and outs
tops of scenes and the bottoms
—the passing moments
My husband.
My husband?

Man
... jealousy ...
It is the green-eyed monster which doth mock
The meat it feeds on. Good God, the souls of all my tribe defend
From jealousy.

Woman
And then by chance—

> *Drums build a rhythm that carries us for a moment.*
> *A **Witch** pulls a handkerchief out of their pocket*
> *wipes their face with it, and drops it on the stage.*

Woman
    (*to Shakespeare*)
This was her first remembrance from the Moor:
My wayward husband hath a hundred times
Woo'd me to steal it; but she so loves the token,
For he conjured her she should ever keep it,
That she reserves it evermore about her
To kiss and talk to. I'll give't Iago:
what he will do with it
Heaven knows, not I;
I nothing but to please his fantasy.
I nothing but to please his—
    (*falling out*)
Is that the line?
It is.
I nothing but to please his fantasy.

An entire person birthed out of a need to please.

> *He interrupts her. It will not be the last time.*
> *Music cuts out. Maybe they have a beat just looking at*
> *each other and nothing happens.*

Man
How now! what do you here alone?

Woman
Do not you chide; I have a thing for you.

Man
A thing for me? it is a common thing—

Woman
Ha!

Man
To have a foolish wife.

Woman
O, is that all? What will you give me now
For the same handkerchief?

Man
What handkerchief?

Woman
What handkerchief?
Why, that the Moor first gave to Desdemona;
That which so often you did bid me steal.

Man
Hast stol'n it from her?

Woman
No, 'faith; she let it drop by negligence.
And, to the advantage, I, being here, took't up.
Look, here it is.

Man
A good wench; give it me.

Woman
What will you do with 't, that you have been
so earnest to have me filch it?

Man
Be not acknown on 't; I have use for it.
Go, leave me.

> *He takes it from her. Could be rough. Could be sweet. It's likely both.*
> *The drummer continues again.*
>
> *Another interruption.*
> *Feedback from the* **Band**. *The* **Band** *bounces a low Bb.*

Woman
He goes.
And then . . .

Desdemona
Hey, have you seen my . . . my . . .

> *Beat.*

The handkerchief?
My handkerchief?
I can't find it.
And he's . . .

Woman
>   (*to audience*)

A scene between Othello and his wife.
They fight.

>   *An abrupt slash from the drums.*

Woman
And then another scene.
>   (*falling to Shakespeare, to* **Desdemona**)

Is my lord angry?
He went hence but now in strange unquietness.

Desdemona
I never gave him cause.

Woman
But jealous souls will not be answer'd so;
They are not ever jealous for the cause,
But jealous for they are jealous: 'tis a monster
Begot upon itself, born on itself.

>   *to the audience*

And then they fight again.
She and Othello
And he. . . .
He hits her.

>   *a slap. A hit from the drums.*

hard.

Desdemona
>   (*falling to Shakespeare*)

My lord, I have not deserved this.

Woman
Good madam, what's the matter with my lord?

II. Emilia 139

Desdemona
With who?

Woman
Why, with my lord, madam.

Desdemona
I have none: do not talk to me, Emilia.
I cannot weep, nor answers have I none
But what should go by water. Prithee, tonight
Lay on my bed my wedding sheets. Remember.
And call thy husband hither.

> *Perhaps the* **Woman** *goes to bring* **Man**. *If so then our* **Desdemona** *has a moment alone with the* **Witches**.

Man
What is your pleasure, madam? How is't with you?

Desdemona
I cannot tell. Those that do teach young babes
Do it with gentle means and easy tasks.
He might have chid me so, for, in good faith,
I am a child to chiding.
Am I that name, Iago?

Man
What name, fair lady?

Woman
He called her "whore". A beggar in his drink
Could not have laid such terms upon his callet.
I will be hang'd, if some eternal villain,
Some busy and insinuating rogue,
Some cogging, cozening slave, to get some office,
Have not devised this slander; I'll be hang'd else.
Why should he call her whore? who keeps her company?
The Moor's abused by some most villainous knave,
Some base notorious knave, some scurvy fellow.

Man
>*(to Emilia)*
>
>Speak within door.

Woman
Some such squire he was
That turn'd your wit the seamy side without,
And made you to suspect me with the Moor.

Man
You are a fool. Go to!
>*(Exits)*

Woman
>*(to audience)*
>
>And then, finally
Just us two.

>*The* **Witches**, **Woman** *and* **Desdemona** *work together, placing freshly cleaned sheets on the bed setting it carefully, diligently.*

Woman
How goes it now? he looks gentler than he did.

Desdemona
He hath commanded me to go to bed,
And bade me to dismiss you.

Woman
Dismiss me!

Desdemona
We must not now displease him.

Woman
I would you had never seen him!

II. Emilia

Desdemona
All's one. Good faith, how foolish are our minds!
If I do die before thee . . . shroud me
In one of ⟨those⟩ same sheets.

> *Beat.*

My mother had a maid called Barbary.
She was in love, and he she loved proved mad
And did forsake her. She had a song of willow,
An old thing 'twas, but it expressed her fortune,
And she died singing it. That song tonight
Will not go from my mind.

> *Instead of finishing her thought* **Desdemona** *launches in to the "Willow Song" a rhythmic, persistent a cappella partly performed in mournful anticipation.*

Song 7: Willow Song

Desdemona	**Witches and Woman**
THE POOR SOUL SAT SIGHING	WILLOW
BY A SYCAMORE TREE,	WILLOW
SING ALL A GREEN WILLOW	WILLOW

HER HAND ON HER BOSOM, HER HEAD ON HER KNEE

THE POOR SOUL SAT SIGHING	WILLOW
BY A SYCAMORE TREE,	WILLOW
SING ALL A GREEN WILLOW	WILLOW

Desdemona
HER HAND ON HER BOSOM, HER HEAD
ON HER KNEE
WILLOW, WILLOW,
WILLOW, WILLOW!

THE FRESH STREAMS RAN BY HER,
AND MURMUR'D HER MOANS
HER SALT TEARS FELL FROM HER,
AND SOFTENED . . .
AND SOFTENED THE STONES
SING!

All
WILLOW, WILLOW,
WILLOW, WILLOW
WILLOW, WILLOW
WILLOW, WILLOW

All
WILLOW, WILLOW,
WILLOW, WILLOW
WILLOW, WILLOW
WILLOW, WILLOW

> *"Willow" finishes, and we are left with a few subtle notes and falling solo lines from the musicians.*

Desdemona
(to Shakespeare)
O, these men, these men!
Dost thou in conscience think,—tell me, Emilia,—
That there be women do abuse their husbands
In such gross kind?

Woman
(falling to Shakespeare)
Yes, a dozen; and as many to the vantage as would
store the world they played for.
But I do think it is their husbands' faults
If wives do fall: say that they slack their duties,
And pour our treasures into foreign laps . . .
Or else break out in peevish jealousies,

Throwing restraint upon us or say they strike us,
Or scant our former having in despite;
Why, we have galls, and though we have some grace,
Yet have we some revenge.
Let husbands know
Their wives have sense like them:
they see and smell and have their palates both for sweet and sour,
As husbands have. What is it that they do
When they change us for others? Is it sport?
I think it is: and doth affection breed it?
I think it doth: is't frailty that thus errs?
It is so too: and have not we affections,
Desires for sport, and frailty, as men have?
Then let them use us well: else let them know,
The ills we do, their ills instruct us so.

Desdemona
Good night, good night!

> *The women say goodbye to each other. It is warm, it is real. And then, our* **Desdemona** *exits the space.*

Woman
   (*to the audience*)
That was the last time I saw her.
My friend.
That was our last scene.
I liked her.

A breath.

When Othello kills Desdemona in the play
the stage direction usually reads—

Desdemona
"He smothers her."

Woman
That's it.
After she is killed, I have a scene with Othello
Our titular character, alone.
It is then that I discover her dead in her bed.
But in the original story that this little play is based on
—because most of Shakespeare's stories are adaptations
bits and imaginings pieced together from
places that existed long before he . . .
In *that* original story
written thirty-nine years before Shakespeare wrote
Othello
Iago and Othello work together to kill Desdemona.

First Witch
They beat her with a sandbag

Third Witch
Break, and collapse the bedroom walls

Second Witch
So that the very walls of the house all fall on her
as if by accident

First Witch
To hide their crime.

Woman
So that it looks like—

> *The* **Man** *interrupts again. Underscoring cuts out.*
> *The two fall into a battle of sorts. They play for real and*
> *for keeps in the following scene.*

Man
    (*to Shakespeare*)
What is the matter?

II. Emilia   145

Woman
O, are you come, Iago? You have done well,
That men must lay their murders on your neck.

Man
What is the matter?

Woman
   (*to audience*)
Disprove this villain, if thou be'st a man:
He says thou told'st him that his wife was false:
I know thou didst not, thou'rt not such a villain:
Speak, for my heart is full.

Man
I told him what I thought, and told no more
Than what he found himself was apt and true.

Woman
But did you ever tell him she was false?

Man
I did.

Woman
You told a lie, an odious, damned lie;
Upon my soul, a lie, a wicked lie.
She false?

Man
Go to, charm your tongue.

Woman
I will not charm my tongue; I am bound to speak:
   (*to audience*)
My mistress here lies murder'd in her bed,—
Villany, villany, villany!
I think upon't, I think: I smell't: O villany!—

I thought so then.
O villany, villany!

Man
What, are you mad? I charge you, get you home.

Woman
Perchance, Iago, I will ne'er go home.

> *With this, something is unlocked in the* **Man**.
> *Something slips out of place, that cannot be set right.*

Man
Come, hold your peace.

Woman
'Twill out, 'twill out: I peace!
No, I will speak as liberal as the north:
Let heaven and men and devils, let them all,
All, all, cry shame against me, yet I'll speak.

Man
Be wise, and get you home.

Woman
I will not.

First Witch
It is here
That the stage direction often reads . . .

First Witch
"Iago offers to stab Emilia"

Woman
That's it.

Desdemona
"Iago offers to stab Emilia."

II. Emilia 147

Woman
But in reality, this moment is more like—
A woman almost making it out the door.
A woman just reaching for her keys
for her car door

Third Witch
A woman going back that last time to get her bag
or her things
or her *child*.

Desdemona
It looks like that last phone call to her sister
that last text to her cousin

Third Witch
or auntie, or mother

All Women
or friend.

First Witch
It looks like the time she had a *hunch*.

Woman
The time she had a feeling
That time she thought to herself—

>   *And then seamlessly, she sings. Gently at first.*
>   *Slowly but surely* **Band** *builds with her.*

Song 8: Too Late to Pay

Woman
I SHOULD'A LEFT YOU, A LONG TIME AGO
I SHOULD'A LEFT YOU, SO MANY AGES

I SHOULD'A LEFT YOU WHEN MY SISTERS TRIED
TO GET ME
SO LONG AGO

Man
Wait.

Woman
(*singing again*)
IF I HAD A LISTENED TO ALL MY FRIENDS
IF I HAD A LISTENED AND COME TO SOME SENSE

Man
Please!

Woman
What. What is it?

> *A breath. Then to audience.*
> *The* **Man** *waits nearby. It is hard for him to do so. He has perhaps had enough for the evening.*

Man
You can't just . . .
You can't just . . .
There is poetry.

Woman
Is violence worth poetry?

Man
Some of these speeches are—

Woman
Sure.
and by the time the curtain comes down
Women are laid out on the f l o o r.

Man
It's not about you.

Woman
Hate is not reserved only for me.
It's for women
and "Turks" and
Many, many others.
This play is just full of hate.
(*to audience*)
And before you assume that's what I think of Shakespeare
That this is a judgement,
—I don't. It's not.
Lemme just take a second and be as clear as possible:
I AM NOT SAYING THAT SHAKESPEARE
HATED WOMEN.
I DON'T KNOW WHO THE FUCK HE WAS
I WASN'T THERE
AND NEITHER WERE ANY OF YOU.
But this play *Othello*?
It has a whole lot of hate.
'Prolly got it for good reasons . . .
but we've been doing it for years.
Watching it for years
and that has a cost.
THAT'S ALL I AM SAYING.
It isn't for free.
the violence we casually receive?
In the news, in these stories?
It goes somewhere.
I think that Shakespeare knew that.
whoever he was.
he was looking
and seeing
and smart enough to capture the fact that
marriage doesn't always have a happy ending.
That in a fearful world,

loving someone different than you can be dangerous
That for sisters
Wives
Friends . . .
Jealousy can get you killed.

Man
—Wait.

Woman
    (*spiteful*)
O-t-h-e-l-l-o.
What a play.
One man feels wronged.
And this man feels that another man
—a man that is different from him—
has wronged him
is *wrongfully* on top of him
And immediately
Before we know what is up and what is down
This "wrongèd man", that's you
You know exactly what to do
how to do it
And who to do it to.
How to make others believe you.
You know the route
You draw the map
You draw the line
A black one.
But it's good.
I mean, it is a good play.
The best. It makes us think.
Does it make us think twice though?
Or does it just make the little corners of us feel seen.
But back to you.
Back to Iago.

Second Witch
> (*as a pompous director*)

"Is Iago a racist?"

Woman

That's what always comes up when working on this play.
> (*the director again*)

Desdemona
> (*as a critic*)

"Is Iago a racist?"

First Witch

Instead of: what is our responsibility
to deal with the violence against women
in this play?

Woman

This play was written in 1603
That is four hundred and twenty-three years ago.
Why is it still so relevant?

Man

That's why it—

Woman

I know, I know
But I just really . . .
I hate that it lasts. That it *will* last.
—Put it in your season and people will flock to it.
Put sexy people in it
Sexy men killing sexy women
People eat that shit up.
Jealousy and racism
Timeless.

First Witch

Priceless.

Woman
Lasted four hundred years
And will certainly last four hundred more.
   (to audience)
Do you know what Othello says on his dying breath?

Man
   (falling to Othello)
Soft you. A word or two before you go.

Woman
You want to do his speech, don't you.
Do you even know it?

Man
I do.

Woman
Go ahead.

Man
   (as Othello. Beautifully)
Soft you. A word or two before you go.
 I have done the state some service, and
 they know't.
 No more of that. I pray you in your letters,
 When you shall these unlucky deeds relate,
 Speak of me as I am. Nothing extenuate,
 Nor set down aught in malice. Then must you speak
 Of one that loved not wisely, but too well;
 Of one not easily jealous, but being wrought,
 Perplexed in the extreme; of one whose hand,
 Like the base Judean, threw a pearl away
 Richer than all his tribe; of one whose
 subdued eyes,
 Albeit unused to the melting mood,
 Drops tears as fast as the Arabian trees
 Their medicinable gum. Set you down this.

And say besides, that in Aleppo once,
Where a malignant and a turbanned Turk
Beat a Venetian and traduced the state,
I took by th' throat the circumcisèd dog,
And smote him, thus.

Woman
And then he—

Man
—and then he stabs himself.

Woman
But what he is saying is

First Witch
remember me as a *good* negro.
Remember me as one of you.
As someone who did your violence
He speaks the right way.
He speaks to be heard.
    (*to* **Man**)
By you.

Woman
And it works.
    (*to audience*)
I guarantee
Whatever production you see
In this moment
you will sit there
and you will weep.
It likely won't be for my cold dead body
Or for Desdemona's.
It will be for him.
When minutes before you watched this man
Smother his own wife.
Or shoot

Or bludgeon
Or whatever dark fancy the director has chosen for the evening.
—You will feel for him.

Man
What about me?
What about Iago?

Woman
You get to live!
Iago gets to live.
Can you believe that?
Your final words are

Man
   (*falling to Shakespeare*)
—Demand me nothing.
What you know, you know.
From this time forth, I never will speak word.

Woman
Unbelievable.
Really.
I mean ladies . . .
You could put all of your might and power into this work
Into the character
Into your little death
But at the end of the day
Everyone in the room is going to be more interested
In this white man's *motive*
Then anything you or any other actress
Could ever do.
For every Tamir Rice
There is a Dylan Roof who gets taken to Burger King.
For every constable Wayne Couzens and Payton Gendron there is a—

Bang.

Before this argument can finish. The **Man** *reveals a gun, and he shoots her. Over the next she begins to bleed. This bleeding does not stop until we are done.*

Man
I'm sorry.
—I'm . . .
I didn't mean it.
really.
I didn't.
It just happened
You were talking and
I had a weapon
on me all this time
it's for the character
but when you were talking just now
. . . you sounded . . .
(((something bothered me)))
I know I'm not supposed to say that out loud.
I'm *supposed* to be listening.
I'm trying to listen
and when things bother me
Even if things hurt me I'm not supposed to . . .
because we need to shift the . . .
It's not my moment.
—there needs to be a . . . *balance?*
But it's just . . .
>   (*to the* **Witches**)

It's so much, you know?
And I'm not sure it's fair to . . .
You can't blame . . .

>   *Beat. She bleeds.*

We've been through so much together
In these plays. All of these plays.

And I see you I do
But it's a lot to take
and I'm not sure how *much* I can take.
how much I'm *supposed* to take.
Because when you look at me like I'm the problem
When you look at me like
Like you hate me
Like you *want* to hate me
I don't understand.
Because this is a play!
it's a
it's a
it's a play
It's *for* play!
It's not for real.
—or some things are real

> *shifting*.

. . . can't we all agree that things that *were* real then are *less* real now?
That things have gotten better?
I don't even really believe that
It's coming out of my mouth and it's shit.
I just . . .
(((I'm sorry.))))
but

First Witch
Stop.

Man
—but she can't

Desdemona
please.

Man
But I—

Second Witch
Stop.

Man
—we . . .

Desdemona and Women
s t o p.

Man

> *Beat.*
> *And then, to her.*

Do you want me to stop?

> *Beat.*

It's going to be okay.
You'll see
Just let me . . .
—Let me
. . . we can . . .
Juliet.
Juliet or Cleopatra or—

Woman
It doesn't matter
what play we do.

Man
We're friends.

Woman
Impossible.

Man
I love you.

Woman
How can you love me
When you are so afraid of me?

Man
I'm not afraid of you.

Woman
Y o u   a r e   a f r a i d   o f   m e.
He is afraid of her.
Poor Iago.
He is so afraid of her truth.

> *Beat. (To audience.)*

But there's nothing that can kill a woman's truth.
So Emilia may not make through Act Five but—

Man
—but you and I?

Woman
You and I—

> *And then she sings our final song of the evening. During this, the* **Man** *cleans her wound and dresses her. He must deal with the blood, and perhaps even reveal the theatrical artifice behind this moment of violence.*
>
> *Somehow, we make it clear that Emilia is gone but this* **Woman** *and* **Man** *will continue on. During this she should do as little as possible, other than breathe and sing. A reconciliation.*

Witches
I SHOULD'A LEFT YOU AND COME TO SOME SENSE
I SHOULD HAVE LEFT YOU AND COME TO SOME
SENSE
OH THEY TRIED TO HELP ME BUT I WAS SO LOST
A FOOL, AND COULDN'T QUIT YOU
IT'S TRUE

> *Lights fade on this little pair.*

END.

Part III: Juliet

I.

*When lights rise our playing space has shifted in time. The **Band** remains but at the center of the room is a playground set and bits of grass breaking through the ground. The **Witches** are strewn about, with microphones in hand doing spells, cat's cradle, hopscotch and playing other games of yesterday.*

They sing a youthful grunge rock song to the audience and each other.
*The **Man** with a pair of headphones moves about the space putting the final touches on a playground set.*

Song 1: Spell

All Witches
I CAST A SPELL ON YOU
ON YOU, ON YOU.
I CAST A SPELL ON YOU
ON YOU, ON YOU.

TO REMEMBER THE DAYS, AND ALL OF OUR
YOUTH!
I CAST A SPELL ON YOU
ON YOU ON YOU!

IT MAKES US ALL MAD
REMEMBERING YOUTH . . .
IT MAKES ALL LOVE
IT MAKES ALL MAD

I CAST A SPELL ON YOU
ON YOU, ON YOU.
TO REMEMBER THE DAYS, AND ALL OF OUR YOUTH

SO HALLELU-JAH
HALLELU
HO HALLELU-JAH
HALLELU

I CAST A SPELL ON YOU
ON YOU, ON YOU.
I CAST A SPELL ON YOU
ON YOU, ON YOU.

... REMEMBER THE DAYS, AND ALL OF OUR YOUTH!
I CAST A SPELL ON YOU
ON YOU ON YOU!

ALL WITCHES
Tonight we sing of a little girl
who didn't get to be a little girl
because little girls don't get to be little girls.
Little Black girls don't get to be little Black girls.
We are gathered here today to sing of that little girl
To Juliet.
—to youth.

> *The **Woman** enters, seeing the **Witches** in their newly girl-sit form tries to play with them.*

Woman
Cool song.

Second Witch
Hi.

Third Witch
Whatever.
Don't talk to us

Woman
—what?

Third Witch
Don't even look at us!

First Witch
We don't want to help you.

Woman
Who says I need your help?

Third Witch
Your hair looks stupid.

Second Witch
 (*laughing*)
Stop it

Third Witch
You obviously need our help.

Second Witch
((((((I like your shoes)))))

Third Witch
No she doesn't.

All
 (*teasing*)
First's the worst,
Second's the best,
Third's the one with the hairy chest!

> *The* **Third Witch** *slugs her in the breast, or pushes her or pulls her hair or does some other demon child delight.*

Third Witch
You want to do *Romeo and Juliet*?

All
Romeo and Juliet?

First Witch
You're not a Juliet!

All
You're not a Juliet!

Woman
can't you help me? Be my sister?
    can't you be my auntie?
        My fr—

Witches
Noooooo
    nooooooo!
too much.
too much!

Third Witch
Deal with your own shit.

All
—and do it alone.

First Witch
You have questions?

All
We don't care.

First Witch
You wanna be in love?

All
Boo hoo hoo!
Boo hoo hoo!

Boo hoo hoo!
You want to do *Romeo and Juliet*?
do it alone.
Do it alone!

First Witch
You want to make it to the end of her story?

All
do it alone!

Woman
Are you spirits?

> *With this the* **Witches** *die of laughter, running about spreading their energy about the room.*

All Witches
    are we spirits whaaaat? ((like she doesn't know?))
Ooooohhhhhhhhhhh. . . ..
      Are we spirits?
    ooohhhhhhhhhhhhhh!!!!
      come on!

Third Witch
Deal with your shit.

All
And do it alone.

Woman
But . . .
Fine.

> *They go. Probably a little bullying on the exit. Playful, but still cuts through.* **Man** *and* **Woman** *are left together. When* **Man** *takes off a pair of headphones*

Woman
Hi.

> **Man**
> How are you?

Woman
How long have you // been

> **Man**
> —Do you like it?

Woman
I love it.

> **Man**
> Thank god.

Woman
. . . How did you even // know?

> **Man**
> ah.
> You told me.

Woman
Did I?

> **Man**
> I think so.
> I thought it could be good for you to try her
> —try the play this way.

Woman
I used to spend so much time here.
—somewhere like here.
We're supposed to do *Romeo and Juliet* now?

> **Man**
> Yeah. Who do you want to play?

Woman
I'd make a righteous Romeo.

> **Man**
> Sorry, he's mine.

Woman
Is he?

> **Man**
> Yeah.

Woman
I can't with Juliet.

> **Man**
> Why?

Woman
Because of time?
Because of who I am?
Because . . . (((boobs?))))

Man
What's wrong with boobs?

Woman
I had breasts by the time I was like 11.
I don't think your typical Juliet can have . . .
It was so horrible.
People started looking at me differently
—they just
You have to start walking different.
Wearing different things
Watching after yourself.
you just . . .
you have to grow up.

Man
Everyone has to grow up.

Woman
. . . sure.

Man
Come here. Just sit here.

> *The* **Man** *brings the* **Woman** *to a little part of their little park.*
> *He sits with her and perhaps encourages some play, or performs some show of youth.*

Man
Close your eyes.

Woman
What are you // why do I

Man
Try to maybe . . .
—just try to think of b e f o r e.

Woman
Before?

Man
Before the ring.
Before the crown.
Before Lady Macbeth
and Emilia . . .

Woman
—That's not really

Man
Before t i m e.

The start
The beginning
Youth.

A moment here.

Not even youth but—

Woman
I can't. I'm so sorry
I don't give good Juliet.

> **Man**
> You make it sound like kink.
> Like something dirty.

Woman
Isn't it?

> **Man**
> Try.

Woman
Really . . . I can't.

> **Man**
> Why not?

Woman
I mean putting all of the . . .
Historical stereotypes assumptions and hyper sexualization
of black women // and girls aside. . . .

> **Man**
> —you sound like a newspaper.

Woman
 . . . and the way people throughout time
have obsessed over Juliet's // virginal . . .

Man
—when you talk like that it's just
gobelygook

Woman
We're too old.
Like you and me?
To be them?
those kids were like 13.

Man
she was twelve.
he was a bit older.
>*Breath.*

just **try.**

Woman
There's something perverse about it.

Man
It's fun.
It's okay for this to be fun too, you know.
>*Beat.*

I dare you.

Woman
Excuse me?

Man
I said, I **dare** you.

Woman
Then you have to show me who you are.

Man
I mean, what do you want to know?

Woman
(testing)
show me who you are.

Man
okay. I will.
> *A moment as they consider what this means.*

Woman
Okay.

Man
—okay?

Woman
I'll do it.
I'll give you Juliet.
I'll give you good Juliet.
—can you guys come back?

> *The* **Band** *returns from their set break with new gear: a few pedals added and other toys. They begin to play "Smoke", a Lo-fi 90s pop indie song.*
>
> **Man** *finds a cube of some light, cheap watery beer and crushes a few beers or does other things with the empty cans that sadly, impresses her.*
>
> *they sing together.*

Song 2: Smoke

Woman
LET'S GO BACK TO '97 BABE
WHEN I PUSHED YOU IN THE ALLEY
I KISSED YOUR BRIGHT RED CHEEKS
YOU WERE SO AFRAID OF ME

GO BACK TO WAY BACK WHEN
WE SMOKED OUT THE WINDOW
27TH FLOOR
NO NET

NO ONE TO CATCH US.
NO ONE TO CATCH US.

Man
GO BACK TO '97 BABE
WHEN I WAS THE BIG FISH
THE KIDS KNEW MY FACE
EVERYBODY KNEW
YOUR NAME
I RAN INTO THE WIND
SNEAKING OUT AND   **Woman**
SNEAKING IN   SNEAKING OUT AND
                               SNEAKING IN
CAN'T TELL ME   NO ONE TO CATCH US
ANYTHING
NO ONE TO CATCH US

Both
NO ONE TO CATCH US.

Woman
SHOW ME ALL THE DIRTY
BOOKS IN THE LIBRARY   **Man and Women**
PUSH ME WAY TOO HIGH   I WILL, FOR ALL OF
UP ON A SWING   TIME
SPIN THE BOTTLE DO   OH . . .
DIRTY THINGS
TO ME

Man
IN THE BURGER JOINT . . .

Woman
IN THE BATHROOM.

Both
DON'T FORGET MY FUCKING *F R I E S*

Both
BROWN EYES, YOU
BEFORE I COULD *LIE*

Both
WE . . . SWEET TIES
SWEET TIES
SWEET, SWEET, SWEET, SWEET
SWEET, SWEET SWEET SWEET
YEAH, YEAH.
SMOKE.

Woman
AND IF I'M NOT SWEET
I MIGHT NOT BE
IT'S FINE BECAUSE RIGHT NOW, RIGHT NOW
I CANT EVEN SAY HER NAME

I'LL TRY TO BE

YOU TRY TO BE
HER NAME
HER NAME
. . . JULIET.

By now the **Man** *has rolled a joint. He offers it to her.*

Woman	
YOU MY ROMEO	
HE	**Man**
DON'T EVER GO.	DON'T EVER GO.
WE . . . SWEET TIES	WE . . . SWEET TIES
SMOKE	SMOKE

Both
YOUR EYES, YOU
BEFORE YOU COULD LIE
WE . . . SWEET TIES
SWEET TIES
SWEET, SWEET, SWEET, SWEET
YEAH YEAH YEAH
SWEET, SWEET SWEET SWEET
YEAH, YEAH, YEAH

> *They each take a puff blowing a little air in each other's faces. It's not sexy, it should be kinda dumb and they should know it's dumb but it is a contract for them both to try to find a youth forever lost.*
>
> *Lights shift.*

II.

> *Lights find our actor who played* **Desdemona**. *She has returned and is now dressed in a stunning, painstakingly femme heritage costume that any of the best Juliets would die to wear.*
>
> *She holds a copy of* Romeo and Juliet *and is now working on the speech for the first time. Perhaps the* **Woman** *mouths along or even tries to speak a few lines with her.*

Shadow Juliet
Gallop apace, you fiery-footed steeds,
Towards Phoebus' lodging: such a waggoner
As Phaethon would whip you to the west,
And bring in cloudy night immediately.
    (*falling to her language and making clear the scansion*)
And-bring-in-cloud-y-night-im-*me*-di-*at*-ly.
    (*trying a different stress*)
And-bring-in-cloud-y-night-im-me-di-*atly*.
Spread thy close curtain, love-performing night,
That runaway's eyes may wink and Romeo
Leap to these arms, untalk'd of and unseen.

> *Lights fall on her, and we are left with the* **Woman** *watching. Until this moment is broken by . . .*
>
> *The* **Man**. *He rummages through a cooler and takes out a can of shaving cream. He takes a box cutter, punctures it and inhales. He puts his thumb over the hole, and offers her one. She declines, but he partakes.*

Woman
I have this visceral memory
Of like every single woman I have ever seen do this role
Like in my entire life.
Do you know what I mean?

Man
I get it.

Woman
I hear their voices.

Man
—It's a big one isn't it.

Woman
I see their stupid little costumes,
((((Okay. I quite like the costumes actually)).

Man
Just find your own way into it.

Woman
It's really hard to unhear like . . .
The way they did it.

Shadow Juliet
Spread thy close curtain, love-performing
night . . .
Leap to these arms . . .

Woman
Voice high,
Eyes wide
The yearning.
The openhearted tragic yearning.
—the girls in school
The young women who received their *dame-hood* in ingenue-ing, you know?
They would be so shocked when they got cast, cast as Juliet.

Shadow Juliet
oh gods, it . . . it's yesyesyesyesyes
it is. Holy yesssssss
I got it. I got the part!

Woman
But none of us other busty matronly tweens were shocked.
None of us other Black girls, brown girls, whatever
"other" kind of girls.
Not at all like duh.
Obviously it's her.
Obviously she's the one.

Song 3: Forever Girl

Shadow Juliet
I GOT IT, I GOT IT
I G-G YEAH I GOT IT!
I GOT IT, I GOT IT
I G-G YEAH I GOT IT!

SHE'S THE ONE SHE'S THE DREAM
SHE'S EVERYTHING,
SHE'S FOREVER GIRL
FOREVER TEEN

YOU LIKE IT WHEN SHE SMILES
SOMETIMES SHE BARELY SPEAKS
THEN WE WAIT AGAIN UNTIL IT'S TIME FOR ME!

SO YOU LIKE WHEN I TALK, WHEN I TALK
THIS WAY
WHEN I LOWER MY EYES AND THEN I LOOK AWAY?
YOU LIKE IT WHEN IT HAPPENS I GOT
NOTHING TO SAY
I GOT NOTHING TO SAY . . .
I GOT NOTHING TO SAY!
SO YOU LIKE IT WHEN THE LIGHT IT JUST
HITS MY EYES
AND YOU SEE YOURSELF THROUGH THE PRISM OF
MY SMILE
YOU LIKE IT WHEN I TELL YOU
THAT YOU'RE ALWAYS RIGHT
IF I COULD STAY THIS WAY THEN, GEE
THAT COULD BE NICE

GUESS WHAT?

I CAN BE NICE, I CAN BE NICE, I
CAN BE NICE
REALLY REALLY REALLY
REALLY NICE!
I CAN BE NICE, I CAN BE NICE, I
REALLY REALLY NICE
REALLY NICE!

> SHE WILL BE FOREVER!
> SHE WILL BE FOREVER!
> JULIET FOREVER!
> JULIET FOREVER!
>
> SHE WILL BE FOREVER!
> SHE WILL BE FOREVER!
> JULIET FOREVER!
> JULIET FOREVER!

Shadow Juliet and Witches
I CAN BE NICE, I CAN BE NICE
REALLY REALLY NICE
I CAN BE NICE
REALLY REALLY REALLY!
I CAN BE NICE, I CAN BE NICE
REALLY REALLY NICE
I CAN BE NICE
REALLY REALLY REALLY

UNTIL THE END OF THE SONG
UNTIL THE END OF THE PLAY!
UNTIL THE END OF THE SONG
UNTIL THE END OF OUR DAYS.

UNTIL THE END OF THE SONG
UNTIL THE END OF THE PLAY!
UNTIL THE END OF THE SONG
UNTIL THE END OF OUR DAYS.

Shadow Juliet
Who are you playing again?
You'll be great.
I'll just be here.
I'll be her
I'll be JULIET forever.
Judi Dench
Norma Shearer
Olivia Hussey
Claire Danes
and me.
((Muah!))

> *As the song ends, the* **Woman** *is left watching our Shadow Juliet as she finishes the revelry. The* **Man**, *stays fixed on the* **Woman.**

Woman
Like I remember thethethe
—like . . . the h e r i t a g e that people didn't even really have the right to.
The nostalgia.
The fantasy.
The protection of that fantasy, for some.
But don't we all fall in love?
Didn't we all have youth?
I was always the maid.
Somebody's maid.
But you, I bet you were Romeo, right?
Come on.

Man
Everyone is somebody's Romeo.

Woman
Exactly. Anyone can be a Romeo,
but not everyone can be a Juliet.

What did they call the other ones?
The other Black girls
The queens who had this role?
They said

> **Man**
> "Romeo wouldn't die for her if she looked like that"

Woman
They call casting a Black Juliet "controversial"

> **Man**
> "foolish"

Woman
"It's not about race, she's just ugly"
They weren't ugly.
They were beautiful.
Like any young woman is.
Some girls get to be girls I guess.
Cute costumes though.

> *A breath as the* **Woman** *watches our Shadow Juliet who takes a break but remains ever in view.*

III.

> *The two fuss about the space and with each other.*
> *Energy and bodies trying to find a state of being from*
> *long ago.*

Man
Do you remember the beginning of the play?

Woman
I'm trying to!
My mind just kind of . . .
—when they first meet at the party
The characters.
that's the beginning for me.

> **Man**
> Because that's the beginning for her.

Woman
No shit.

> **Man**
> don't be nasty.

Woman
I know there's a lot that goes on before
Before you meet me
Before you. Meet // her

> **Man**
> The play begins with a fight.

Woman
Actually the play begins with a warning.

Man
>*(falling to Shakespeare)*

Two households, both alike in dignity
In fair Verona, where we lay our scene
From ancient grudge break to new mutiny,
Where civil blood makes civil hands unclean.
From forth the fatal loins of these two foes
A pair of star-crossed lovers take their life.

Whose misadventured piteous overthrows
Do with their death bury their parents' strife.
The fearful passage of their death-mark'd love,
And the continuance of their parents' rage,
Which, but their children's end, nought could remove,
Is now the two hours' traffic of our stage;
The which if you with patient ears attend,

Both
What here shall miss, our toil shall strive to mend.

>*A shift here. Like it always does Shakespeare's words somehow make the stakes of our wold bigger.*

Man
Middle class.

Woman
—what?

Man
I guess you could say, that I was middle class.
Or my family was.

Woman
Right.
I guess you could say I was middle class too
But in America everyone says they are middle class

Even when you're at the bottom of that middle class
Hanging on to it by bare threads
Which I guess we were.
and were you into women? Girls?

> **Man**
> Early and fast.
> What do you miss?

Woman
My goodness
About being young?

> **Man**
> —about being *younger*.

Woman
I miss not knowing.
Like, I didn't know anything
and I *thought* I knew everything.

> **Man**
> First crush?

Woman
I dunno if I can answer that.

> **Man**
> why not?

Woman
It's too risky!!

> **Man**
> Mine was a sop 2 in choir.

Woman
choir boy!?
Beat.

Mine was a Jewish kid
Thick hair.
Lived near the Starbucks.
((('Oh god I shouldn't be // saying this))
Yes, I know.
And anyways.
that was my first crush.
But my first *kiss* was a girl actually.
Second grade.
Bathroom.
Catholic school.

> **Man**
> really?

Woman
Mm hmm.
—but just
Oh my gosh
There was so much heat.

> **Man**
> what do you mean?

Woman
Like . . .
growing up in the city.
Thinking that "the city" made me tough, you know?
crushing on somebody
beefin' with somebody
Getting the A
But wanting The A+
Oooh, I *wanted* that A+.

> **Man**
> Nerd.

Woman
Still do.

basketball
track
choir
I just did the most.
I just had to keep moving.
If I kept moving
Maybe I could make some money
If I kept moving
Maybe things would be better for me
Then they were for
Some of the other young women in my family
you know.

>*Beat.*

Okay so the beginning.
The fight.

Man
Sampson and Gregory.
House of Capulet

Woman
Oh.
Juliet is a Capulet.
So the drama comes from my side.
Those are my cousins?

Man
—with swords and bucklers.

Woman
Show me.

>*With this prompt the **Man** falls into Shakespeare's world and action. He is impressive. His language is clear his choices strong as he embodies different players.*

Man
A dog of the house of Montague moves me.

A dog of that house shall move me to stand. I
will take the wall of any man or maid of Montague's.
'Tis all one. I will show myself a tyrant.
When I have fought with the men, I will be civil
with the maids; I will cut off their heads.

Woman
(falling to Shakespeare)
The heads of maids?

Man
Ay, the heads of the maids, or their maidenheads.
Take it in what sense thou wilt.

Woman
(immature)
They must take it in sense that feel it.

Man
so they fight, and our parents fight . . .

Woman
I don't care about any of this.

Man
Maybe you should.
It's a pretty good brawl
six-character fight at least.

Woman
Oh you like fights?

Man
. . . like stage fights.
sure.

Woman
Stage fights guy.
Mkay.

Have you ever fought anyone?
For real?
With your bare hands?
Seems important if you're going to play Romeo.

Man
> (*hardens*)
> I certainly have

Woman
Okay.
So this story
— this fight between my family and yours?

Man
> It's one of many that has spilled out into the streets
> disturbed the public
> its peace.
> Then you know, new scene! My mom
> she like . . .
> —she asks Benvolio my cousin and like my best friend
> if he's seen me
> and I saw him
> but I ran away from him.
> and I went through a breakup
> and I'm like super super sad.
> Like . . .
>   sullen.

Woman
But I don't wanna get into that.

Man
> why?

Woman
—because I don't really care.
Let's just get to where my story starts.

Man

But the beginning sets up the power.
The structure.
Juliet by all accounts
—given who she is
and the time she is living in
. . . she's powerless.

Woman

I'll let you know
if I think she's powerless.

Man

Okay. But, even she's not going to stay a child for long.
In the beginning of the play
she's being married off.
There are two men

Woman

One is my father
and he says . . .

Desdemona

My child is yet a stranger in the world.
She hath not seen the change of fourteen years.
Let two more summers wither in their pride
Ere we may think her ripe to be a bride.

Woman

This grown adult man
a man of power.
a "prince".
Is asking for her—Juliet—my hand in marriage?
An all the way grown-up adult man
has no business marrying a twelve-year-old
(((because nobody has any business marrying
a twelve-year-old)))
He says

> **Desdemona**
> (*as Paris*)
> Younger than she are happy mothers made.

Woman
And my father says

> **Desdemona**
> And too soon marred are those so early made.

Woman
—he says . . .

> **Desdemona**
> But woo her, gentle Paris, get her heart;
> My will to her consent is but a part.
> This night I hold an old accustomed feast,
> Whereto I have invited many a guest

Man
See, even she isn't safe.

IV.

> *The **Man** fastens something in the space to make a pull-up bar. At will, he does pull-ups and push-ups throughout the next sequence and other tests of strength and masculinity. Somehow the movement allows him to fall into a curious state of juvenility.*

Man
Get young.

Woman
—what?

Man
Do it.
Go.

Woman
Fine. Okay.

Man
Let's go together. Reid fire. Okay?

Woman
. . . okay.

Woman	**Man**
Xena.	*South Park.*
X-Men.	*EastEnders.*
The Simpsons.	same.
Gogurt	We didn't have that here.
Lunchables	that's not food it's plastic.
Like pizza.	Way too much pizza.

Man
What about music?

Woman
Rock.

> **Man**
> Pop.

Woman
I was so into rock.
The radio.

> **Man**
> Walkman.

Woman
Indie rock.

Woman
Nine Inch Nails.
I had a boombox tucked under my bed.
And put my earbuds into it
and fell asleep listening to it every night.

> **Man**
> (*radio voice*)
> . . . you're listening to q101

Woman	**Man**
I couldn't handle being alone.	I always wanted to be alone.

I wanted to drink
but was too scared.

> **Man**
> —you didn't drink?

Woman
No, not really.
Not till later.
My . . . a couple people
Women in my family they . . . a bit too much.
So I was scared.

Man
When I was fourteen I had to be taken to the hospital.
for drinking.

Woman
Oh no.

Man
So much throwing up.
blacking out.

Woman
So you were a reveler?

Man
I was a reveler.
always falling in love and falling out of love
and trying to fit in
but knowing I was different. And everyone in my village knowing I was
different, and running away from ghosts like
my family.
—and
like all the firsts, you know?

Woman
Yeah.

Man
likkkkeeeeeeeeee the first kisses and the touching and the fingers
and the smell. Like women. The smell of women.
And the hhhhhhhhhhh

Woman
—hhhhhhhh

BOTH
humping?

Woman
yeah.
In the back of a car
the library
the burger joint . . .

> **Man**
> the burger spot, again?

Woman
A lot of seminal times were spent there.

> **Man**
> First dance?

Woman
Homecoming.
Grinding like GRINDING

> **Man**
> Let's do it

Woman
I dunno.

> **Man**
> come on.

Woman
Uhhh

> **Man**
> I know.
> I'm awkward.

Woman
No you're not.

> **Man**
> I *was* awkward.
> a stranger in my own body.
> I don't miss that, wondering why people were looking at me
> at my stupid face.
> That's why I did drugs.

Woman
The drugs light you up.

> **Man**
> —the drugs light you up.

Woman
So what happens next?

> **Man**
> In rrrrrrromeo and juliet?

Woman
Yeah.
after the fight
after the proclamation
after my parents discuss selling me off.

> **Man**
> Well, there's a party of course.

Woman
Shakespeare and his parties.

> **Man**
> and that's where we meet.

Woman
that's cool.
Let's do that.

Man
Yeah. I think so too.
to be able to meet again?
to meet your love again for the first time?
to do it all again, really.
Like I said, blank slate.
So you have to go.

Woman
Okay.

Man
And I'll be waiting here outside your house.
outside the party.

Woman
and then we . . .
and then it happens?

Man
yeah.

Woman
Okay.

> *The **Woman** goes. As she does we hear the thump thump of a subwoofer, one you could hear outside a club. Muted but still, a siren song. The **Man** alone reveals a mask from his bag. It is not overly ornate: something of older times, and something of today.*
>
> *The **Witches** reenter as revelers Benvolio, Mercutio and all. Also masked. One pulls out a purple baggie filled with pills and tosses it to **Man**. He crushes a few, dips his pinky into the powder and leaves it for those who wish to partake.*
>
> *The space lights up and we hear a reprise of "Spell".*

> *The guitarist and bassist take their instruments or acoustic versions to a new area in the space. As the drugs and party favors taken begin to take hold, our Shadow Juliet Returns.*

Song 4: Spell Reprise

Witches
I CAST A SPELL ON YOU, ON YOU ON YOU
I CAST A SPELL ON YOU ON YOU ON YOU
TO REMEMBER THE DAYS AND
ALL OF OUR YOUTH
I PUT A SPELL ON YOU.

> **Man**
> (*knighting the* **Witches**)
> Enter Mercutio, Benvolio
> with five or six Maskers, Torch-Bearers.
> Give me a torch: I am not for this ambling;
> Being but heavy, I will bear the light.

Third Witch
(*as Benvolio*)
Nay, gentle Romeo, we must have you dance.

> **Man**
> Not I, believe me: you have dancing shoes
> With nimble soles: I have a soul of lead
> So stakes me to the ground I cannot move.

First Witch
(*as Benvolio*)
You are a lover; borrow Cupid's wings,
And soar with them above a common bound.

> **Man**
> I am too sore enpiercèd with his shaft
> To soar with his light feathers, and so bound,

I cannot bound a pitch above dull woe:
Under love's heavy burden do i sink.

First Witch
And, to sink in it, should you burden love;
Too great oppression for a tender thing.

Man
Is love a tender thing? it is too rough,
Too rude, too boisterous, and it pricks like thorn.

Second Witch
If love be rough with you, be rough with love;
Prick love for pricking, and you beat love down.

Romeo
I dreamt a dream tonight.

Second Witch
And so did I.

Man
what was yours?

Second Witch
That dreamers often lie.

Man
In bed asleep, while they do dream things true.

Second Witch
(*as Mercutio*)
O, then, I see queen Mab hath been with you
She is the fairies' midwife, and she comes
In shape no bigger than an agate-stone
On the fore-finger of an alderman,
And she hath been with me too.
(*falling to her own language*)
When she came, she showed me

Images of our time.
Children shot in cars
Fire in the countryside.
Men marching two by two
drones whizzing by, while you eat your food.
She makes mothers act crazy
Like they forgot and don't remember
What it is to be a girl.
To have a dream.
That they can help their daughters make another choice.

I have seen queen Mab
She gives men ideas at night
That become consequences by day
Chaos for the rest of your days.

She runs through lovers' brains, and then they
dream of love.
Through women's minds and their lives disappear
Their ambition
Their power.
Smoke.

I have seen queen Mab.
She rings like drums in my ear
I start, I wake, I breathe
I sleep again
There are drums in my ear
I start, I wake, I think, I breathe
I wake
The world's the same
Might as well sleep again.

Man
Peace, peace.
Thou talk'st of nothing.

Second Witch
I have seen queen Mab.

Witches
She makes us all mad.
Remembering youth . . .
She makes all love
She makes all mad

I cast a spell on you
On you, on you.
To remember the days, and all of our youth

I cast a spell on you
On you, on you.
I cast a spell on you
On you, on you.

> *As the* **Witches** *sing they summon both Shadow Juliet and* **Woman** *again we see them from the* **Man***'s perspective: a strange mangled collage of* **Women***.*

Man
   (*falling to Shakespeare*)
Some consequence yet hanging in the stars
Shall bitterly begin his fearful date
With this night's revels, and expire the term
Of a despisèd life closed in my breast
By some vile forfeit of untimely death.

> *This odd party comes to an end. The* **Witches** *take their exit as the party is over. Before the* **First Witch** *leaves, they snap causing light to shift, and focus on the* **Woman** *now in the space.*

Man
   (*somehow seeing her differently*)
O, she doth teach the torches to burn bright!

Woman
What?

Man
Nothing. It's time.
It's time for us to meet.

Woman
I know
I can't really wait anymore
I want it to happen now.
So

Man
So, you come in

Woman
—and you spot me across the room.

> *As the pair assume their positions a light pull to them, focusing, and grounding them with each other.*

Man
and I say
(*falling to Shakespeare*)
O, she doth teach the torches to burn bright!
It seems she hangs upon the cheek of night
As a rich jewel in an Ethiop's ear—
Beauty too rich for use, for Earth too dear.
So shows a snowy dove trooping with crows
As yonder lady o'er her fellows shows.
Did my heart love till now? Forswear it, sight,
For I ne'er saw true beauty till this night.
What's the matter?

Woman
I feel silly.
Like when people play this part do they feel little silly?
I just
I always wanted to hear those words
said to me on stage.

Part III: Juliet

Man
Everyone wants to be beautiful

Woman
A snowy dove? And Ehtiop's ear?
Of course, but to whose standards?
It just seems small to me now.

> **Man**
> You're lying.
> love and beauty are not small to you now.
> (*taking her hand*)
> If I profane with my unworthiest hand
> This holy shrine, the gentle sin is this:
> My lips, two blushing pilgrims, ready stand
> To smooth that rough touch with
> a tender kiss.

Woman
Good pilgrim, you do wrong your hand too much,
Which mannerly devotion shows in this;
For saints have hands that pilgrims' hands do touch,
And palm to palm is holy palmers' kiss.

> **Man**
> Have not saints lips, and holy palmers too?

Woman
Ay, pilgrim, lips that they must use in prayer.

> **Man**
> O then, dear saint, let lips do what hands do.
> They pray: grant thou, lest faith turn to despair.

Woman
Saints do not move, though grant for prayers' sake.

Man

Then move not while my prayer's effect I take.

He kisses her.

Thus from my lips, by thine, my sin is purged.

Woman

Then have my lips the sin that they have took.

Man

Sin from my lips? O trespass sweetly urged!
Give me my sin again.

Woman

(*laughing*)
You kiss by th' book.

Man

—what?
We're doing *Romeo and Juliet*. We have to kiss.

Woman

That's fine
at that age I used to be able to do that and nothing but that for hours
It's kind of disgusting really
But being here with you it reminds me of this time when
My mom, she—

A witch appears, however this time she is not just a witch. She is a mother. Perhaps a natural black bob wig and a classy bag is slung over a shoulder headed out the door and to a job in which she is not seen and will work until death.

Woman

Oh shit.
It's happening.

Man
what?

Woman
Hide.
— just hide

Man
Why?

Woman
It's my mom
I remember, it now
she left for work
and I thought the coast was clear
So I let this kid sneak upstairs
And she totally saw him go up.
But she didn't break up our fun
Instead, she waited until we were done and then
After he left was waiting for me by the elevator and . . .

First Witch
(*as mom*)
you need to stop playing around.
You don't have a lot of time!

Woman
I mean . . .
I thought school
That my youth was for *me*.
But it turns out . . .

First Witch
—school is just a way out.

Woman
Get smart, sure.

First Witch
—Get a degree, even better.

Second Witch
But a husband?

> *And then with a bit of magic, the other two witches pop their heads out and join* **First Witch**—*they are now all her mother, all in the same wig and outfit.*

All Witches
DINNG DING DING!
That's the ticket!
That's the lottery.
I love you baby girl but . . .
find a way out!
Because I can only help you so much.

Third Witch
I love you and I'm trying.

First Witch
I'm helping and I'm trying
But
Find a way out!
A husband?
A man?
The degree of course . . .
But a man?

Second Witch
And which man you ask?
Oh any, dear.
May he be good
May he be nice
But above all
May he be a way out!

*The **Witches** each give her a motherly goodbye.*
A hug, a kiss. A wag of the finger. They fix
her up a bit.

Man
that's so
It's so different than the way I . . .

Woman
Is it?
Moms worry for little boys too.

Man
yeah, but not for us to settle down.
not immediately.
It's not like, settle down or *die*.
That wasn't really the message // I got.

Woman
Well then what? What did // you

Man
If anything I was just told
to . . .
be strong.
and it was okay to be bad, sometimes.
like if I got into it.
boys will be boys, they said.
be smart
be clever
be strong.
be a man.

Beat.

But what is that?

*The **Woman** nods, leaning in a bit as music rises softly to transition us into the next moment.*

V.

> *The **Man** prepares for the balcony scene.*
> *He does this with excitement and quite a lot of nerves.*

Woman
Okay wait wait wait
Should I get up higher?

> **Man**
> yeah, if you can.

Woman
Like, here?

> **Man**
> That's good.

Woman
wait—

> **Man**
> just lemme know when you're ready.

Woman
Alright, I'm ready.

> **Man**
> (*to Shakespeare*)
> He jests at scars that never felt a wound.

Woman
That's your first line, for the balcony scene?

> **Man**
> Yeah.

Woman
What does that even mean?

Man
It's hard without context. So just
turn away or something, and then come back.
   (*she does*)
But soft, what light through yonder window breaks?
It is the East, and Juliet is the sun.
Arise, fair sun, and kill the envious moon,
Who is already sick and pale with grief
That thou, her maid, art far more fair than she.
Be not her maid since she is envious.
Her vestal livery is but sick and green,
And none but fools do wear it. Cast it off.
It is my lady. O, it is my love!
O, that she knew she were!
She speaks, yet she says nothing. What of that?
   (*falling out*)
talk to yourself
say something to yourself.

Woman
   (*mumbling*)
. . . okay. Like—

Man
Her eye discourses; I will answer it.
I am too bold. 'Tis not to me she speaks.
Two of the fairest stars in all the heaven,
Having some business, do entreat her eyes
To twinkle in their spheres till they return.
What if her eyes were there, they in her head?
The brightness of her cheek would shame
those stars
As daylight doth a lamp . . .

Woman
Ay me.

> **Man**
> She speaks.
> O, speak again, bright angel, for thou art
> As glorious to this night, being o'er
> my head,
> As is a wingèd messenger of heaven
> Unto the white-upturnèd wond'ring eyes
> Of mortals that fall back to gaze on him
> When he bestrides the lazy puffing clouds
> And sails upon the bosom of the air.

Woman
> (*to audience*)

Okay.
here we go.
Here it is
> (*to* **Man**)

O Romeo, Romeo, wherefore art thou Romeo?
Deny thy father and refuse thy name,
Or, if thou wilt not, be but sworn my love,
And I'll no longer be a Capulet.
'Tis but thy name that is my enemy.
Thou art thyself, though not a Montague.
What's Montague? It is nor hand, nor foot,
Nor arm, nor face. O, be some other name
Belonging to a man.
What's in a name? That which we call a rose
By any other word would smell as sweet.
So Romeo would, were he not Romeo called,
Retain that dear perfection which he owes
Without that title. Romeo, doff thy name,
And, for thy name, which is no part of thee,
Take all myself.

Man
I take thee at thy word.
Call me but love, and I'll be new baptized.
Henceforth I never will be Romeo.

Woman
My ears have yet not drunk a hundred words
Of thy tongue's uttering, yet I know the sound.
Art thou not Romeo, and a Montague?
   (*falling out*)
How camest thou hither, tell me, and wherefore?
The orchard walls are high and hard to climb,
And the place death, considering who thou art,
If any of my kinsmen find thee here.

Man
With love's light wings did I o'erperch these walls,
For stony limits cannot hold love out,
And what love can do, that dares love attempt.
Therefore thy kinsmen are no stop to me.

Woman
If they do see thee, they will murder thee.

Man
Alack, there lies more peril in thine eye
Than twenty of their swords. Look thou but sweet,
And I am proof against their enmity.

Woman
I would not for the world they saw thee here.

Man
I have night's cloak to hide me from their eyes,
And, but thou love me, let them find me here.
My life were better ended by their hate
Than death proroguèd, wanting of thy love.

Woman
By whose direction found'st thou out this place?

> **Man**
> By love, that first did prompt me to inquire.
> He lent me counsel, and I lent him eyes.
> I am no pilot; yet, wert thou as far
> As that vast shore washed with the farthest sea,
> I should adventure for such merchandise.

Woman
O gentle Romeo,
If thou dost love, pronounce it faithfully.
Or, if thou thinkest I am too quickly won,
I'll frown and be perverse and say thee nay,
So thou wilt woo, but else not for the world.
In truth, fair Montague, I am too fond,
And therefore thou mayst think my havior light.
But trust me, gentleman, I'll prove more true
Than those that have more coying to be strange.
I should have been more strange, I must confess,
But that thou overheard'st ere I was ware
My true-love passion. Therefore pardon me,
And not impute this yielding to light love,
Which the dark night hath so discoverèd.

> **Man**
> Lady, by yonder blessèd moon I vow,
> That tips with silver all these fruit-tree tops—

Woman
O, swear not by the moon, th' inconstant moon,
That monthly changes in her circled orb,
Lest that thy love prove likewise variable.

> **Man**
> What shall I swear by?

Woman
Do not swear at all.
Or, if thou wilt, swear by thy gracious self,
Which is the god of my idolatry,
And I'll believe thee.

> **Man**
> If my heart's dear love—

Woman
> Well, do not swear. Although I joy in thee,
> I have no joy of this contract tonight.
> It is too rash, too unadvised, too sudden,
> Too like the lightning, which doth cease to be
> Ere one can say "It lightens." Sweet, good night.
> This bud of love, by summer's ripening breath,
> May prove a beauteous flower when next we meet.
> Good night, good night. As sweet repose and rest
> Come to thy heart as that within my breast.

> **Man**
> O, wilt thou leave me so unsatisfied?

Woman
What satisfaction canst thou have tonight?

> **Man**
> Th' exchange of thy love's faithful vow for mine.

Woman
I gave thee mine before thou didst request it,
And yet I would it were to give again.

> **Man**
> Wouldst thou withdraw it? For what purpose, love?

Woman
But to be frank and give it thee again.
My bounty is as boundless as the sea,

My love as deep. The more I give to thee,
The more I have, for both are infinite.

> *A moment as our guitarist plays a tag from "Smoke".*
> *They process.*

Woman
That is
That is crazy.

> **Man**
> It's fast.

Woman
desire and hormones.

> **Man**
> I did a lot of things because of desire and hormones.

Woman
And then because of this
Because we fall in love
The entire play . . . ?
All the killing and fighting?

> **Man**
> yeah.

Woman
It's like there's a gun to my head.
I don't know about you
But the rashest decisions I've ever made
weren't because of love
They were made because I had no other way out.
No couch to crash on
No job
No father to help me

Mother too tired to guide me
And everyone else speaking language
I didn't understand

Man

or not speaking to me at all.
Like, I can count on my hand the amount of times
—in the times it mattered—an adult offered me
anything.
or took the time to talk to me.
to understand.
You just had to figure everything out on your own.

Woman
(to Shakespeare)
Deny thy father and refuse thy name,
Or, if thou wilt not, be but sworn my love,
And I'll no longer be a Capulet.
'Tis but thy name that is my enemy.
The place death, considering who thou art,
(finding her own language)
do you hear that?
These kids are running.

Man
—For their lives.
Their families offer them nothing but war.
So this love, their love, is—

Man and Woman
—a way out.

Woman
Yeah.
It feels like a way out.

Man
It starts with the parents.
Isn't that what they say?
I never even have scenes with mine.

Woman
Mine barely talk to me.
That feels like now.

Man
Sure.

Woman
We aren't talking to our youth.
We aren't working to make a better world for them.
What do they do when they need to figure things out?

Man
go on the internet.

Woman
Oh god.

Man
It's all so violent isn't it?
All of it.
my character falls in love and
because of a feud, a brawl
kills your cousin who kills my cousin.

Beat.

Growing up I was told never to do that
Boys will be boys
I could get into it now and then
but there was a line.
Except when you try to be the thing
Be the boy.
Be the man.

You're playing fast and loose in a group
of other men
It's a thin line.
and there are times where I could, where I can feel it
wanting to cross that line.
I have to be honest about that.
Beat.

But if I can be the hero
I'd prefer to be the hero
I prefer to just do that.
and stay away from it all.

Woman
Okay.

Man
(*after a time*)
I don't miss the recklessness.

Woman
I do.

Man
(*shift*)
Okay it's time.

Woman
For what?

Man
We just . . .
We just have to be in love now.

Woman
—but I'm not ready.

Man
That's just the way it is.
We sang our little songs
had our little moment
and now it's time.

> **Woman**
> But I said I'm **not ready.**
> I just got to know her
> . . . my little Juliet.

Man
They don't have time.
They don't have the luxury.

> **Woman**
> Well I want to take the fucking time.
> Stop pushing me
> See that?
> See how you just take power?
> *(hardening)*
> What a tragedy this girl is.
> ## Why would anyone want to be Juliet?
> This girl is not well.
> . . . she is so unwell
> and no one is helping her
> no one is helping him either.
> Both of them.
> But I get it. Playing Juliet is like getting a stamp
> You get a Juliet on your resume
> And you are worthy
> You are youth.
> But you know what?
> I don't think I want to go back to my youth.
> . . . like
> I don't wanna die . . .
> But I don't want to go back either.

Because if I had another shot
I don't know if I would be smart enough to avoid all
those close calls.
> *Beat.*

So why would anyone want to do this play?

Man
because even if we might not want to go back
we want to remember.
> *Beat.*

What do *you* remember? About the end?

Woman
In the end?
It is crowded.
We are in a tomb.
bodies
Ancestors

> **Man**
> and us.
> then I awake
> there you lay in my arms.
> and I think you're . . .
> I think you're dead
> So I . . .
>> *They assume this position. It takes a moment to find but they work on it together.*
>
> . . . and with wife dead in my arms
> I take my life.

Woman
—Wait
I told you.
I don't give good Juliet.

Man
But you do.
you did.

Woman
— and once the world tells you not to be something
It's easier not to even try.
because
I feel . . . I mean I feel . . .

Man
It doesn't matter what *she* feels.
the end is coming

Woman
But I'm not ready
and it's your fault.

Man
What are you talking about?
it takes
—it took
both of us
We went through it all.
We talked about our families
about society
our stupid lovers
our—
so that's it.
that's it.

> *From the* **Man***'s pocket, he reveals a final drug. He takes a final hit, one last dose of poison and falls to Shakespeare's words.*

Ah, dear Juliet,
For fear of that I still will stay with thee,
And never from this palace of dim night

Depart again. Here, here will I remain
With worms that are thy chamber-maids. O, here
Will I set up my everlasting rest,
And shake the yoke of inauspicious stars
From this world-wearied flesh. Eyes,
look your last!
Arms, take your last embrace! And, lips, O you
The doors of breath, seal with a righteous kiss
A dateless bargain to engrossing death!
Come, bitter conduct
come, unsavory guide,
Here's to my love!
Thy drugs are quick. Thus with a kiss I die.

A moment here
With this, our final song begins, sung easefully.

Song 5: Last Light

Man
LET'S GO
WHERE THERE
ARE NO . . .
    MORE STARS
NO EYES
NO WATCH
NOWHERE
NOWHERE

Man
LET'S GO
WHERE THERE
ARE NO . . . MORE STARS!
NO EYES
NO WATCH
NOWHERE
NOWHERE

Witches
AH

Man
NO HOME
HO HEART
NO WAR
NO ART
NO ROAD
NOWHERE TO GO!

Witches
AH

Man
LAST BREATH
LAST SIGHT
LAST LIGHT
YOUR EYES
DON'T GO
DON'T GO
DON'T GO
DON'T GO
<<DON'T GO>>

> *And then, he dies. It is as real a death*
> *as the actor can muster. After this death, she awakes.*
> *A moment as she deals with his body, and herself.*

Woman
That's it.
He's gone.
And now . . .
Do I have to follow?
But how?
   (*to Shakespeare*)
What's here? A cup closed in my true love's hand?

Poison, I see, hath been his timeless end.
O churl drunk all and left no friendly drop
To help me after. I will kiss thy lips.
Haply some poison yet doth hang on them
To make me die with a restorative.

> *She tries. She touches her face to his, but there is no poison left.*

Woman
None left.
. . .
What am I supposed to do?
(((but)))
Think of all the things
That this girl
could do with her life?

> *She finds his gun. The same from before which wounded her as Emilia. With this, the* **Witches** *return. She looks to them for help.*

Woman
Oh good you're here.
I'm so happy you're here.
You've come to help me right?

Witches

. . .

Woman
No jokes?
No warnings?

Witches

. . .

Woman
Just please.
Help me.

Witches

. . .

> *As she weighs her final decision, we fade to black and in darkness, we hear a final shot.*
>
> *The* **Witches** *offer a final round of Hallelu. Perhaps light lingers on them a bit as our final witnesses of the scene.*

Witches
Hallelujah . . .
                    hallelujah
Hallelujah
                    hallelujah
Hallelujah
                    hallelujah
Halle . . . lujah . . .

IV. Richard III

> *We begin with the band playing a majestic 6/8 rhythm. Lights find our **Band** dressed to kill looking better than ever and ready for the evening's proceedings. If performed in succession, they will have witnessed and been part of three different Shakespearian worlds, and by now have a knowing sensibility about them. They play freely, as most rules have already been broken.*
>
> *A procession begins as the **Witches** move about the space, reinvigorating the first spell they cast. They sing to each other and the audience as we make our way into our final story.*

Song 1: Hallelu Redux

First Witch
1 . . . 2 . . . 3 . . . 4 . . .

> *With this the **Witches** speak in time speaking rhythmically with each other and the audience.*

First Witch
ONCE UPON A TIME THERE WAS A BLACK GIRL
WHO MADE IT VERY FAR
IN THE GREAT WHITE WORLD
SHE CLIMBED TO THE TOP
AND EVEN THERE SHE COULDN'T STOP
CUZ WHEN SHE LOOKED DOWN
SHE SAW A WHOLE LOT.

Second Witch
. . . A WHOLE LOTTA PROBLEMS

First Witch
A WHOLE LOTTA LIES!

Second Witch
... A WHOLE LOTTA DREAMS

Third Witch
—AND SISTERS WHO DIED

First Witch
STORY AFTER STORY
THEY ROBBED US OF OUR GLORY

Third Witch
THEY ROBBED US OF OUR GLORY

All
SO SHE TRIED AND SHE TRIED
AND SHE TRIED AND TRIED.
AND WE TRY AND WE TRY
BAAAAAABY WE TRY

Third Witch
BUT AFTER ALL THESE PLAYS
THESE GIRLS LOSE THEY LIVES
IF THE WOMEN KEEP LOSING
YOU ASK YOURSELF WHY?

First Witch and Witches
THE WHY BECAME A LETTER
THAT WHY BECAME A FIRE.
FIRE GREW AND GREW
CLIMBED UP HIGHER

BUT WHAT'S AT THE TOP
OUR SISTER CAN'T STOP!
ONE LAST STORY TO GO
BEFORE THE BALL DROPS!

> *With a gesture from the* **Witches** *music shifts again and they change up the flow. Their voices move heavenly together. Divine. A perfect trio of harmony.*

All
HALLELUJAH! HALLELU
HALLELUJAH! HALLELU
HALLELUJAH! HALLELU
HALLELUJAH . . .

Woman
No.

First Witch
What do you mean no?

Woman
Just . . . . .no.

Second Witch
I think she missed us.

Third Witch
She did.

First Witch
Look. You did good sweetie.
You did all your parts.
Lady Macbeth, Emilia, Juliet.
All the dancing and talking . . .

Woman
—acting.

First Witch.
Yeah. That.
You did as best as you could.

Woman
You think you can do better?

First Witch
Of course I could, but I'm not trying to.
See, I made my peace.

Woman
Is that what peace looks like?

First Witch
Who do you think we are boo? Vapors?
Sweetie we are you.

Second Witch
Were you.

Third Witch
Will always be, *you*.

First Witch
We've been Juliets, nurses, queens
and sistas you pass on the street.
Woman in pain, chorus girl, babymomma—

Second Witch
sisters, whores

Third Witch
Waiting for the promotion
Waiting for the doctor's appointment

First Witch
stuck in bad shoes

Third Witch
Cut in line and shuffling behind

All Witches
 . . . and

Woman
 (*overlapping*)
—and?

Third Witch
—and sometimes it's okay to enjoy the part you have.
It may not be his part
It may be small . . .
But at least you don't have to carry all of this.

Woman
But why not?
—Why not his part?

Third Witch
You want to fight four hundred years?

> *The* **Woman** *takes a moment—it is brief but her doubt slips through.*

Second Witch
Awwwww whats-a-wrong?

Third Witch
You need little positive reinforcement?

Second Witch
—well boo hoo.
We been trying to support you up here
but one can only take so much.

First Witch
Look.
The scene was set
The characters met
It was Romeo and Juliet!

Second Witch
Such a good one!

First Witch
It's not like his character got to see the ripe old age of retirement

The sun didn't set rosy and cozy on his horizon
In *Romeo and Juliet* he dies . . .

Third Witch
He does!

First Witch
The kids die, the cousins die . . .

Woman
So whether queen or wife
Or woman at the beginning of her story
None of us can make it to the end?

First Witch
What are you really fighting?
Because every story has an end.

Second Witch
If Shakespeare was alive right now
and you could ask him one question,
what would it be?

Woman
    (*after a time*)
How did he know?
How did he know that these stories would last forever?
That we would be
Contending with them
Surviving them
regurgitating them
over and over.

gling to get more for themselves would be an
always-type-of-struggle.
Somehow, he captured something
at the core of all of who *we* are.
And all I know

Is that these stories are connected
to me and to you
to my aunt
and your mom
to your husband
your school
the movies you watch
and the way we speak
And carry ourselves
The very way we frame each other and understand each other.
And something is just wrong.
And that something can't be solved by rewriting these plays
It can't be solved by rewriting history
Because you can't rewrite history.
So how did he know?

Woman.
I think
The problem is love.
I keep obsessing about power
But all these people, these characters
It's love.

> *The **Band** begins the intro to "For the Lost Ones", a mix between soul and an electronic. It grows to underscore the following sequence. With this we begin our most ambitious costume change yet as **Woman** and **Witches** will begin dressing themselves for **Richard III** on stage.*
>
> *For **Woman**, we will take our inspiration from women of Hip Hop who fearlessly blend masculinity and femininity—red flowing hair and and oversized pieces.*

First Witch
I barely remember the face of Frank
the man who kept my aunt full of liquor.
But I do remember her last days

She was so pretty.
They called her Cocoa
because her skin was like cocoa.
I called her that too.
We were in the attic.
That's where she stayed
on and off again near the end.
One of my last memories of her
She was holding a stack of books, and she was smiling.
I can't remember why I went up to see her that day
But I liked being up there with her.
I didn't understand why she had such a hard time
Because she was fabulous to me.

Third Witch
"I'm going back to school one day"

First Witch
She said . . .

Second Witch
"See all this?
There's so much more out there."

First Witch
A few days before she died she decided to get her hair done.
It was curly and free.
She never liked to get her hair done
She always did it herself.

Third Witch
But she had been in and out of the hospital

Second Witch
—and feeling low.

First Witch
So she got her hair done.
Silky.
Curly.
Black Farrah Fawcett.

All
Yess / laid out / Yes she did / . . . beautiful.

First Witch
When she died
They didn't even need to style it for her.
just laid her out.
I don't remember Frank.
And she was plenty in love with him.
But I do remember her books.

Third Witch
When I think of my cousin
I don't think of the man she ran off to Florida with.
A man she met online
A man she had never met in person before
and someone none of us would ever meet.
I hadn't heard from her in months
And then there was a ring on her hand in the photos.
Some time after a hurricane was coming
I kid you not
They had been living in Florida
and a hurricane was coming that was so bad
they had to leave where they were staying.
And this man called and said . . .

Woman
"You should come get her."

All
Because we aren't taking her with us.

Third Witch
It took so much to get her back.
When she got out of the hospital the last time
she just kept saying
I'm going to travel the world
I'm gonna travel the world . . .

Second Witch
When I think of my mother
I don't think of why she never remarried
Why she never even prioritized it.
I just think of how much she wanted to get her degree.
How much it matters to her to be valued
to be treated with respect.

We fall deeper into "For the Lost Ones".

Song 2: For the Lost Ones

(Reference: Sullen Ground by Mt Kimbie) BPM 105

Woman
THE PROBLEM IS LOVE
IT AIN'T SENT FROM ABOVE
NO!

I'M HOLDING BACK NONE
I'M GONNA GET SOME
FOR THE LOST ONES.
FOR THE LOST ONES.

Witches
IT DOESN'T MATTER HOW YOU TRY TO
RATIONALIZE
VENGEANCE IS UNJUST AND WE WON'T JUST GET
BEHIND
RICHARD THE MAN, HE WALKS A BAD, BAD LINE
THERE IS NO LIGHT SIDE
WRONG SIDE

Witches
OOO
OOO

Woman
GONNA MAKE MYSELF INTO SOMEONE TODAY
A MAN WHO PLAYS THEIR GAME
AND KNOWS THEIR WAYS
I WON'T WANT TO SEE REASON
I JUST WANT WHAT I WANT
AND AS FOR LOVE, I WANT NONE!

Woman	**Witches**
I WON'T TRY TO	IT DOESN'T MATTER
	HOW YOU TRY TO
	RATIONALIZE
RATIONALIZE	VENGEANCE IS
	UNJUST
	AND WE WON'T JUST
	GET BEHIND
	RICHARD THE MAN,
	HE WALKS A BAD, BAD
	LINE
	THERE IS NO LIGHT
	SIDE
	HE'S ON THE WRONG
	SIDE

Here music shifts into a reprise of "If Knowledge Is Power", our opening incantation for the series. Driving hip-hop and RnB.

Woman
WHAT'S THE DIFFERENCE 'TWEEN
WHAT YOU'RE TOLD
AND WHAT YOU KNOW?

Witches
LET ME TELL YOU WHAT I KNOW
TELL YOU WHAT I KNOW!

Woman
WHAT'S THE DIFFERENCE 'TWEEN
WHAT YOU'RE TOLD
AND WHAT YOU KNOW?

Witches
LET ME TELL YOU WHAT I KNOW
TELL YOU WHAT I KNOW!

Woman
CAN YOU REALLY REAP WHAT YOU SOW?
PLANT YOUR ROOTS DEEP
OR YOU'LL HAVE NOWHERE TO GROW
AND THE LONG LINE ON MY LEFT PALM MEANS

ALL
UNREQUITED LOVE!

Woman
AND WITHOUT LOVE
WITHOUT LOVE
ALL I HAVE IS . . .

All
NOW!

All
NOW!
(falling to Shakespeare)
Now is the winter of our discontent
Made glorious summer by this son of York.

Third Witch
. . . uh oh.

Woman
And all the clouds that lourèd upon our house
In the deep bosom of the ocean buried.

Third Witch
Here we go.

> *The* **Man** *draws near, jumping into Richard's opening speech.*

Man and Woman
Grim-visaged war hath smoothed his wrinkled front

Woman
Wait.
I'm going to play him.

Both
Grim-visaged war hath . . .

Woman
I said I will be him.
And you will be she

Man
She.

Woman
Queen Elizabeth

Third Witch
The Duchess of York

First Witch
Lady Anne

Woman
You will be the women
Because I don't have any more she's in me.
If that's okay.
   (*to audience*)

And I don't mean any disrespect.
Of course I'm not a man
And of course I don't know what it's like to live in a body
that doesn't walk the way everyone else's body walks.
That can't move the way the world expects one to move.
But I do know what it feels like to be in body that causes
people to turn away.
I have seen a woman threaten to sick her dog on my
own mother
I have been spat at and so

Second Witch
It's not the same.

Woman
I know it's not the same.
but
Listen—

> *In an effort to convince him, she employs the **Band**.*
> *Music rises to a confident glam rock number that would*
> *make David Bowie blush.*

Song 3: Idol

Woman
ALL OF OUR IDOLS ARE OVERDOSING OR DEAD
ALL OF OUR ICONS ARE GONE IN THE HEAD!
FILLERS AND BLOCKERS TO NUMB ALL THE NOISE
BY THE WAY THINGS LOOK
IT'S NOT A BAD PLAN
NO, IT'S NOT A BAD PLAN
IT WASN'T WHAT WE HOPED FOR . . .
BUT HERE WE ARE!

Witches
OOO!

THE GODS AND THE GODDESSES	**Witches**
ARE TURNING THEIR EYES	TURNING THEIR EYES
WE'RE RUNNING ROUND FORGOT HOW TO EMPATHIZE	JUST CAN'T DO IT!

Woman
STILL, IT'S NOT THAT FAR AWAY

All
NO IT'S NOT THAT FAR AWAY!

Woman and Witches
IT'S GETTING CLOSER AND CLOSER AND CLOSER
AND CLOSER AND . . .
IT'S GETTING CLOSER AND CLOSER
AND CLOSER
AND CLOSER **AND** . . .

Woman
I'LL BE THE BOY AND YOU BE THE GIRL
KIDS THESE DAYS
THEY DON'T CARE!

I'LL BE THE BOY
AND YOU BE THE GIRL
MAYBE WE'LL FEEL SOMETHING
MAYBE WE'LL LEARN!
BUT THE CLOTHES LOOK GOOD ON YOU
YOU MUST ADMIT

WITCHES AND WOMAN
THE CLOTHES LOOK GOOD ON YOU
YOU MUST ADMIT!

> *Music tucks under a moment as the two check in.*

Woman
How do you feel?

Man
Like you care.

Man	**Witches and Woman**
(falling to song)	
ALL OF OUR IDOLS ARE	REST IN PEACE BABE!
OVERDOSING OR DEAD	
ALL OF OUR ICONS ARE	SUCH A SHAME!
GONE IN THE HEAD	
I'LL TRY IT YOUR WAY	
BUT, I WON'T WEAR A DRESS	

Witches and Women
YOU CAN PLAY A WOMAN AND NOT WEAR A DRESS
A GIRL AND STILL NO DRESS
JUST A HEART BEATING, BEATING
IN THE CHEST

Witches	**Man**
JUST A HEART BEATING, BEATING	JUST MY HEART!
IN THE CHEST!	JUST A HEART!

Man
YOU BE THE BOY
AND I'LL BE THE GIRL
KIDS THESE DAYS, THEY DON'T CARE!

YOU BE THE GIRL AND I'LL BE THE BOY
MAYBE YOU'LL LEARN SOMETHING
MAYBE YOU'LL WIN
BUT THE STORY'S GOT TO
END—DOESN'T IT?

All
THE STORY'S GOT TO
END—DOESN'T IT?

All
THE GODS AND THE GODDESSES ARE TURNING
THEIR EYES
THE GODS AND THE GODDESSES ARE TURNING
THEIR EYES

> *The song finishes and the* **Woman** *separates from the group a bit. Perhaps she applauds along with the audience, or another gesture as she attempts to keep the story going.*

Woman
   (*to audience*)
Great.
That was great.
I'm going to continue now, if that's alright.
Because while I liked that song
I don't like that it *took* a song to get us here.
Each time I tried to work on this moment
Each time I drafted this.
I would ask myself . . .

First Witch
How do I get him to be *her*.

Woman
I asked myself . . .

Third Witch
—How do I get him to play her part?

Woman
Because it didn't make sense to me any other way.
It didn't make sense to me for US
The Black us
The brown us
The queer us
To play all the parts.

Second Witch
. . . we might have enjoyed that a bit more

Woman
I mean, that would be an incredible show
if you're out there and want to make that show
please do it.
But for me it doesn't make sense
Because I just can't erase you.
you are him
I don't understand these stories without you and me.
so I asked myself

Witches and Woman
How are we going we do this?

Man
Why don't you just ask me?
Why can't we figure it out together?

Woman
  Beat.
I mean honestly, I can't
Can you . . .
Can you just. . . .
Can you be she?
Because
I am officially over all these girls y'all.

Witches
I heard that. / We get it. / yup

Woman
Each and every one
Every Ophelia, the lady from *Winter's Tale*,
All of them.

I don't want to be any of them!	**Witches**
I'm not auditioning	yup / exactly.

Woman
I'm not making a backstory

Witches
correct!

    First Witch
Get someone else to do it.

Woman
Because I don't want to be reminded of their endings.
And once I realized I was over them
Once I realized that I might not even enjoy playing them
And once I realized that maybe there's nothing to reclaim about them . . .
I thought to myself . . .
    (*to* **Man**)
I would look good in your shoes.

Man
You *would* look good in my shoes.
I tried to tell you that a while ago.

> *With this the* **Man** *helps get her into the final bit of her costume. Or perhaps he adjusts her, to help her find a masculinity she hasn't yet discovered.*

Man
Okay.
So you want me to play the victims?

Woman
Who said that all the women are victims?

Man
They suffer.
Is that it?
You want me to suffer?

Woman
. . . . . .

Man
That's ridiculous.

Third Witch
Sorry to interrupt but . . .
You wouldn't be the only one to suffer.
Richard doesn't just come for the women
He comes for everyone.
Men
Women
Children
Legacy
Crown
Establishment.

Woman
That sounds very good to me.

All Witches
—Wait . . .

Woman

(growing unlikeable)
No.
I need everyone and everything.
The whole story because
Like I said
I have no more she's in me
So. Can we just do that now?
Like **now.**
Okay look.
I know we're all a little unused
unpracticed
Perhaps even uncomfortable with Black women asking for what they want
And not just asking but actually expecting results . . .
but let's just hop to it, can we?

A moment as for the first time, the **Witches** *do not comply. A turning point.*

Woman
Like now.
No more sixteen
No more princess
No more wife
No more queen
Now.
Now!
    (falling to Shakespeare)
Now is the winter of our discontent
Made glorious summer this son of York
And all the clouds that lour'd upon our house
In the deep bosom of the ocean buried.
Now are our brows bound with victorious wreaths,
Our bruised arms hung up for monuments,
Our stern alarums chang'd to merry meetings,
Our dreadful marches to delightful measures.
Grim-visag'd War hath smooth'd his wrinkled front;
And now, instead of mounting barb'd steeds
To fright the souls of fearful adversaries,
He capers nimbly in a lady's chamber
To the lascivious pleasing of a lute.
    (finding her own language)
It actually . . . the speech really rolls off the tongue
So easily it's a little surprising
Because I get it
This is a man who hates the time he is living in.
It's not *his* time
It's not his way.
    (to audience)
This fake liberal moment we are all in?
I mean I don't even know what woke means anymore
I'm sick of having to explain to people that there is nothing wrong with it

There is nothing wrong with WAKING UP
With BEING AWAKE
With reparations
And the right to ones own body
And education
After a while you just start to feel crazy—do you know what
I mean?
You start believing that something is wrong with you that
You are misshapen and not shap'd for sportive tricks,
    (*to Shakespeare*)
That I as a Black woman was not
made to court an amorous looking glass;
I, that am rudely stamp'd, and want love's majesty
To strut before a wonton ambling nymph;
I, that am curtail'd of fair proportion,
Cheated of feature by dissembling nature,
Deform'd, unfinish'd, sent before my time
Into this breathing world, scarce half made up,
(And that so lamely and unfashionable
That dogs bark at me as I halt by them)—
Because I have had a dog bark at me as I walked by
On a police leash
Its owner waiting for my reaction.
    (*to Shakespeare*)
Why I, in this weak piping time of peace,
Have no delight to pass away the time,
Unless to see my shadow in the sun
And descant on mine own deformity.
And therefore, since I cannot prove a lover
To entertain these fair well-spoken days,
I am determined to prove a villain

Second Witch
Okay, I'm for it!

Woman
—and hate the idle pleasures of these days.
Plots have I laid, inductions dangerous,

By drunken prophecies, libels, and dreams,
To set my brother Clarence
   (*to* **Third Witch**)
—you. You're gonna be him.

Third Witch
—wait . . .

Woman
—and the King
In deadly hate the one against the other;
And if King Edward be as true and just
As I am subtle, false, and treacherous,
This day should Clarence closely be mew'd up,
Dive, thoughts, down to my soul; here
Clarence comes.

> *The* **Man** *turns his attention to the* **First Witch**. *For the first time, they are allies. Underscoring shifts to a pulsing chime as the* **Third Witch** *becomes Clarence. She is stripped a bit, perhaps shoes come off or whatever she needs to shed so that she is grounded. The* **First** *and* **Second Witches** *become guards leading her to the Tower—a prison.*

Man
You're up.

Third Witch
I'm up with what?

Man
Clarence.

Man, Second Witch, First Witch
—her brother.

244 All Is But Fantasy

First Witch
(falling into character)
The brother of Richard III . . . ?
. . . Fought beside him in The War of the Roses
Family favorite.
Next in line for the crown.

> *We begin "Clarence in the Tower" a fierce a cappella like one sung by Donald Vail's Choraleers.*

Song 4: Clarence in the Tower

First Witch
UP

> **Second Witch**
> UP

>> **Third Witch**
>> UP

First Witch
WAY

> **Second Witch**
> WAY

>> **Third Witch**
>> . . . WAY

All
HIGH . . .

First Witch
IS

All
CLARENCE!

Second Witch
... CLARENCE IN THE ...

Woman and First Witch
TOWER!

All
TOWER!

> *The song kicks in, heavy and confident, it is a callback to MF DOOM and dark melodic hip hop of an earlier time.*

Woman, First Witch, Second Witch
HA HA HA HA HA HA HA HA HA HA!

Third Witch
BEFORE I STEP INTO MY PART
LET ME SAY ...

I BEEN ROOTING FOR YOU

BUT YOU SEEM A LITTLE LOST

YOU TALK A LOT OF TALK
AND YOU GIVE A LOT OF SHADE

	All
NOW WHAT'S THIS ROLE YOU PLAY?	PLAY!
WHAT'S THIS ROLE THAT YOU PLAY?	SILLY LITTLE GAME

WANNA BE BAD WOLF
GET BACK FOR OLD DAYS?

YOU CAN'T WIN MY GAME
WITH THE SAME OLD WAYS

All Witches

DON'T ACT A FOOL FOR A DOLLAR

FOR A KISS, FOR A MAN

CAN'T DO LIKE THEY DO!

CAN'T ACT A FOOL FOR A CROWN

FOR A HUSTLE, FOR THE SCENE

Third Witch
IF WE'RE SISTERS AND ALL THAT . . .

IT'S SIMPLE TO ME.

All Witches

UP . . . WAY HIGH IS CLARENCE TOWER!	**THIRD WITCH** CLARENCE . . . IN THE TOWER!

Third Witch
(*to* **Second Witch**)
Are you going along with this?

Second Witch
For now.
I don't think we we're getting anywhere before.
At least as Richard she sees the world for for what it is.
To be frank I wasn't down for all
the romance.
It's cute but there's too much work to do.

    Beat.

An eye for an eye
That's what they say.

Third Witch
But whose eye?
> *Beat.*

Anyways
Set the scene.

Second Witch
A prison of sorts.
And you've had a terrible dream.
> (*falling to Shakespeare*)

Why looks your Grace so heavily today?

Third Witch
O, I have passed a miserable night,
So full of fearful dreams, of ugly sights,
That, as I am a Christian faithful man.
I would not spend another such a night
Though 'twere to buy a world of happy days,
So full of dismal terror was the time.

Second Witch
What was your dream, my lord? I pray you tell me.

> *A new section rises in the song, a dizzying waltz that fuses with patient and sturdy gospel. Our* **Third Witch** *stays in focus as she recounts her vision. Is she higher than us? Very separate from us? A spiraling moment of memory, dream and premonition.*

Third Witch
MY DREAM?
MY DREAM?
METHOUGHT I'D...
BROKEN FROM THE TOWER
I WAS HEADED HOME AT LAST
BUT HOME HAD BEEN SOLD.
ALL GONE!

248 All Is But Fantasy

	Woman, Witches, Man
AND NO ONE CALLED MY NAME	NO ONE CALLED MY NAME!
NO SISTERS ... NO BROTHERS!	OH GOD OH GOD!
REMEMBERED HOME!	HOME!
I DREAMED A BLACK WOMAN WAS TO BE PRESIDENT	I LOOK I REACH I WALK I BREATHE I
BUT THEY CUT HER DOWN THE SAME	I BREATHE, I DREAM, I SEE
NO ONE REMEMBERED HOME! ONE REMEMBERED HOME!	NO ONE REMEMBERED NO HOME, NO ONE REMEMBERED HOME!

(falling to Shakespeare and then her own language)

Third Witch

And methought ... what pain it was to drown,
What dreadful noise of waters in my ears,
What sights of ugly death within my eyes.
Methoughts I saw a thousand fearful wracks,
I saw a woman who looked like me
Except she turned her back.
Betrayed me.
She gave up on our dreams.
I saw a thousand men, my brothers that fishes gnawed upon,
Smoking on the corner
Caged
out the yard
No hope
No way
Knives in hand.
guns in hands that should have clasped within them

IV. Richard III 249

Wedges of gold, great anchors, heaps of pearl,
Inestimable stones, unvalued jewels,
But instead . . . all our people
scattered in the bottom of the sea.
Methought . . . what a pain it is to drown.

> *A breath.*

O God my soul is heavy
And I would fain sleep!

> *With this, the* **Witches** *return as the angelic choir.*

First Witch
UP

> **Second Witch**
> UP

>> **Third Witch**
>> UP

First Witch
WAY

> **Second Witch**
> WAY

>> **Third Witch**
>> WAY

>>> **All**
>>> HIGH . . .

First Witch
. . . IS

>> **All**
>> CLARENCE!

All
AND HIS DREAM!

> *With this, our Clarence sleeps. The* **Second Witch** *steps apart from the others becoming The Keeper; a watcher of men's last moments alive. Music rises again as our* **Second Witch** *is joined by the* **First Witch**. *The two become murderers sent to kill Clarence, but they can barely get through their bit. The following is a clown act of sorts.*

Second Witch
What, shall I stab her as she sleeps?

First Witch
Art thou *afraid*?

Second Witch
Not to kill her, having a warrant,
but to be damned for killing her, from the which
no warrant can defend me.

First Witch
Remember our reward when the
deed's done.

Second Witch
(noticing Clarence)
Soft, she wakes!

Third Witch
(waking)
In God's name, what art thou?

First Witch
A man, as you are.

Third Witch
How darkly and how deadly dost thou speak!

Second Witch
There's nothing wrong with a bit of darkness babe.

First Witch
She didn't mean it that way.

Second Witch
In what way did she mean it?
Honestly!
All this "black moor, dark, evil, bad" language is tired.

Third Witch
Your eyes do menace me. Why look you pale?

Second Witch
. . . Just stab her babe.

Third Witch
(*putting up a fight*)
Who sent you hither? Wherefore do you come?

Second Witch
To, to, to—

Third Witch
To murder me?

> **Both**
> Ay. / unfortunately . . . yes.

Third Witch
Are you drawn forth among a world of men
To slay the innocent? What is my offense?
The deed you undertake is damnable.

Second Witch
(*to First Murderer*)
What shall we do?

Woman
(from offstage)
Can you come on!

Third Witch
Relent, and save your souls.

First Witch
Relent? No. 'Tis cowardly and womanish.
    (stabs her)
Take that, and that.
If all this will not do,
I'll drown you in the Malmsey butt within.

> **Second Witch**
>   *(breaking character)*
> I'm sorry but
> That's a hilarious line.
>
> **First Witch**
> Isn't it?
>
> **Second Witch**
>   *(oafish and exaggerated)*
> "I'll drown you in the Malmsey butt within!"
>   *(cackling)*
> Like what is a Malmsey butt!
> Are we pirates?
>   *(stabbing)*
> Arggggh take that and that!

> *With this our* **Third Witch** *has officially lost all her desire for supporting our* **Woman**, *a marked change from how she started her journey. Perhaps she goes through with the playing of being murdered and then rolls from one place to the next to become our next slain body: King Henry the Sixth.*
>
> *The* **Second** *and* **First Witches** *as murderers carry her to our* **Man**, *now fully changed to play*

*Lady Anne. It may be theatrical to change as
little as possible about him. What's most marked is that
he no longer occupies a natural position
of power.*

Our new "She" approaches the body of our
Third Witch *and our world is transformed
into that of a funeral.*

Third Witch
    (*to audience*)
There are many players in Shakespeare's worlds
who don't agree with the story.
"Citizens" in *Julius Caesar*
"The People" in *Coriolanus*
the fool in *King Lear*, animals and nature herself.
When the tides are about to change
we all feel it.
We may try to ignore it, push it down
maintain our routines and safety . . .
But we all have to be honest about when we get the feeling
  . . . that the change upon us
might not be good.
    (*to the ensemble*)
Give us the speech please.

    Underscore changes to a reprise of "Ghosts of Yesterday".

Man
    (*as Lady Anne*)
Set down, set down your honorable load,
If honor may be shrouded in a hearse,
Whilst I awhile obsequiously lament
Th' untimely fall of virtuous Lancaster.
Be it lawful that I invocate thy ghost
To hear the lamentations of poor Anne,
Wife to thy Edward, to thy slaughter'd son
Stabbed by the selfsame hand that made these wounds.
Lo, in these windows that let forth thy life

I pour the helpless balm of my poor eyes.
More direful hap betide that hated wretch
That makes us wretched by the death of thee
Than I can wish to . . .
Wolves, to spiders, toads,
Or any creeping venomed thing that lives.
If ever he have child, abortive be it,
Prodigious, and untimely brought to light,
Whose ugly and unnatural aspect
May fright the hopeful mother at the view,
And that be heir to his unhappiness.
If ever he have wife, let her be made
More miserable by the death of him
Than I am made by my young lord and thee.
Come now towards Chertsey with your holy load,
Taken from Paul's to be interrèd there.
They take up the bier.
And still, as you are weary of this weight,
Rest you, whiles I lament King Henry's corse.

> *Enter* **Woman** *as Richard, Duke of Gloucester. There is a deeper commitment to the villainy of Richard in her gate, posture, voice and even appearance.*

Woman
Stay, you that bear the corse, and set it down.

Man
What black magician conjures up this fiend
To stop devoted charitable deeds?

Woman
(*to the* **Witches***, falling to Shakespeare*)
Villains, set down the corpse or, by Saint Paul,
I'll make a corpse of *she* that disobeys.

Second Witch
My lord, stand back and let the coffin pass.

Woman
Unmannered *dog* . . .

> *Music shifts to "The Recipe". A rolling, quirky funk number.*

Woman
BACKUP SINGER
STAY IN YOUR PLACE
UP OUT THE WAY
  (falling to Shakespeare)
Advance thy halberd higher than my breast,
Or by Saint Paul I'll strike thee to my foot
And spurn upon thee, beggar, for thy boldness.

Song 5: Recipe

First Witch
SISTA GOT THE ITCH
AND THEN SHE SAW HER FIRST PLAY
SHE READ A LI'L SCRIPT
SHE TURNED THE PAGE AFTER PAGE

BURNIN' IN HER HEAD
THE PLAYERS DANCE AND SWEAT AND PLAY
NOW I BEEN DEALIN'   **All**
WITH HER MESS   PLAYS
FOR FOUR WHOLE PLAYS!

First Witch	**All**
YOU CANNOT ACT THIS WAY	HEY!
AND YOU WON'T GET AWAY	HEY!
VILLAINS MAY HAVE THEIR DAY	

All
WE ALL END UP INSIDE THE SAME
THE SAME, THE SAME
THE SAME COLD GRAVE . . .

First Witch
SHE READ ABOUT A QUEEN AND THEN SHE
SHE DRANK IT ALL UP
AND WE BEEN DEALIN' WITH HER MESS
FOR FOUR PLAYS!

All
SHE READ ABOUT A KING AND THEN SHE
DRANK IT ALL UP
AND WE BEEN DEALIN' WITH HER
FOR FOUR WHOLE PLAYS!

First Witch	**All**
(*to the Music Director*)	
WE SAY PREACHER!	PREACHER!
WE NEED YOUR HELP TODAY	

All
GET SOME SOME HOLY WATER
THAT SHE CAN TAKE!

FIRST WITCH	**All**
WE SAY PREACHER!	PREACHER!
COME TAKE THIS GIRL AWAY	
OR ELSE I MIGHT FORGET MY	
CHRISTIAN WAY!	
I SAID	PREACHER!
COME TAKE THIS GIRL AWAY	
GOTTA SAVE HER SOUL	
'FORE THERE'S NOTHING LEFT TO SAVE!	

First Witch
PUT A SISTA IN A SUIT
AND LOOK WHAT YOU GET
A POWER-HUNGRY WOMAN
AS BAD AS IT GETS

Second Witch
PUT A WOMAN IN A SUIT
AND THEY'LL RUN A WHOLE MILE

Third Witch
PUT A WOMAN IN A SUIT
THE COUNTRY LOSES STYLE!

Second Witch	**All**
(*to the Music Director*)	
WE SAY PREACHER!	PREACHER!
WE NEED YOUR HELP TODAY	

All
GET SOME SOME HOLY
WATER THAT SHE CAN TAKE!

Second Witch	**All**
WE SAY PREACHER!	PREACHER!
COME TAKE THIS GIRL AWAY	

All
OR ELSE I MIGHT FORGET MY
CHRISTIAN WAY!

First and Third Witch
SHE READ ABOUT A QUEEN AND
THEN SHE
SHE DRANK IT ALL UP

All Witches
AND WE BEEN DEALIN' WITH HER MESS
FOR FOUR PLAYS!

Third Witch
SHE READ ABOUT A KING AND THEN
SHE DRANK IT ALL UP

All Witches
AND WE BEEN DEALIN' WITH HER
FOR FOUR PLAYS!

> *Our* **Man** *looks to the women who despite tiring of the* **Woman**, *do not give Lady Anne aid.*

Man
    (*to the* **Witches**)
What, do you tremble? Are you all afraid?
Alas, I blame you not, for you are mortal,
And mortal eyes cannot endure the devil.

Woman
Sweet saint, for charity, be not so curst.

Man
Foul devil, for God's sake, hence, and trouble us not,
For thou hast made the happy Earth thy hell,
Filled it with cursing cries and deep exclaims.
O Earth, which this blood drink'st, revenge his death!
Either heaven with lightning strike the murderer dead,
Or Earth gape open wide and eat him quick,
As thou dost swallow up this good king's blood,
Which his hell-governed arm hath butcherèd.

Woman
Lady, you know no rules of charity,
Which renders good for bad, blessings for curses.

Man
Villain, thou know'st nor law of God nor man.
No beast so fierce but knows some touch of pity.

Woman
But I know none, and therefore am no beast.

Man
O, wonderful, when devils tell the truth!

Woman
More wonderful, when angels are so angry.
Vouchsafe, divine perfection of a woman
Of these supposèd crimes to give me leave
By circumstance but to acquit myself.

Man
Vouchsafe, defused infection of a man
Of these known evils but to give me leave
By circumstance to curse thy cursèd self.

Woman
Fairer than tongue can name thee, let me have
Some patient leisure to excuse myself.

Man
Fouler than heart can think thee, thou canst make
No excuse current but to hang thyself.

Woman
By such despair I should accuse myself.

Man
And by despairing shalt thou stand excused
For doing worthy vengeance on thyself
That didst unworthy slaughter upon others.

Woman
Say that I slew them not.

Man
Then say they were not slain.
But dead they are, and, devilish slave, by thee.

Woman
I did not kill your husband.

Man
Why then, he is alive.

Woman
Nay, he is dead, and slain by Edward's hands.

Man
In thy foul throat thou liest. Queen Margaret saw
Thy murd'rous falchion smoking in his blood,
The which thou once didst bend against her breast,
But that thy brothers beat aside the point.

Woman
I was provokèd by her sland'rous tongue,
That laid their guilt upon my guiltless shoulders.

Man
Thou wast provokèd by thy bloody mind,
That never dream'st on aught but butcheries.
Didst thou not kill this king?

Woman
I grant ye, yea.

Man
Dost grant me, hedgehog? Then, God grant me too
Thou mayst be damnèd for that wicked deed.
O, he was gentle, mild, and virtuous.

Woman
The better for the King of heaven that hath him.

IV. Richard III   261

Man
He is in heaven, where thou shalt never come.

Woman
Let him thank me, that holp to send him thither,
For he was fitter for that place than Earth.

Man
And thou unfit for any place but hell.

Woman
Yes, one place else, if you will hear me name it.

Man
Some dungeon.

Woman
Your bedchamber.

> **Witches**
> . . . yoooo . . . / I'm shook / that was actually really smooth /

Man
Ill rest betide the chamber where thou liest!

Woman
So will it, madam, till I lie with you.
—But, gentle Lady Anne,
To leave this keen encounter of our wits
And fall something into a slower method . . .

> *The* **Band** *plays a reprise of "Dark World" and "I For You".*

Song 6: Dark World Reprise / I For You Reprise

Man
This scene is bananas.
I'm sorry.

Woman
Always has been.
You're only noticing it now
Because you have to play her.

Man
. . . Maybe.
I had friends who worked on this part.
in school.
I remember them racking their brains
toiling line after line.
Trying to make it make sense.

Woman
I killed your husband
I killed your father.
and now I have to woo you.
You know, for the crown.
What's so complicated about that?

Woman
IT WAS A DARK WORLD WHEN WE MET
WE WERE BORN WE WERE BORN TO IT
BEFORE WE SET FOOT ON THIS EARTH
IT WAS ABLAZE
IT WAS ABLAZE

KING AND QUEEN AND SYSTEMS RAIN
WE MUST FALL, WE FALL INTO IT
I CAN BE KING THAT'S WHAT THEY SAY
CAN WE MAKE CAN WE MAKE IT?

Man
I'LL ALWAYS BE RIGHT
I'LL ALWAYS BE YOURS

Woman
I WON'T STAY ON MY SIDE

Man
I'LL NEVER CRAWL ON ALL FOURS

Woman
IF YOU BEND A LITTLE BIT
THEN I'LL BEND A LITTLE BIT

Man
IF YOU CAN CHANGE

Woman
I WON'T CHANGE

Man
YOU'RE MY MONSTER
AND I'M YOURS TOO
THE WATER'S TOO DEEP ON BOTH SIDES

Both
THE WATER'S TOO DEEP ON BOTH SIDES
BECAUSE IT'S I FOR YOU
AND WE WILL SEE THIS THROUGH
BECAUSE IT'S I FOR YOU
AND WE WILL SEE THIS THROUGH
BECAUSE IT'S I FOR YOU
AND WE WILL SEE THIS THROUGH

Man
I'LL ALWAYS BE RIGHT
I'LL ALWAYS BE YOURS

Woman
I WON'T STAY ON MY SIDE

Man
I'LL NEVER CRAWL ON ALL FOURS

>   *A breath as they double back into Shakespeare's text.*

Woman
It's your beauty.
>   *(falling to Shakespeare)*
Your beauty is the cause.
Your beauty, that did haunt me in my sleep
To undertake the death of all the world,
So I might live one hour in your sweet bosom.
>   *(to her own words)*
Do you like that?
Do you like being called beautiful?

Man
Don't do that.

Second Witch
He liked it.

Third Witch
He did.

Man
Stop.

Woman
>   *(to Shakespeare)*
It is my day, my life.

Man
Black night o'ershade thy day, and death thy life.

Woman
what's wrong with the black night
The dark shade?

Man
I would I were, to be revenged on thee.

Woman
It is a quarrel most unnatural
To be revenged on him that loveth thee.

Man
It is a quarrel just and reasonable
To be revenged on him that killed my husband.

Woman
He that bereft thee, lady, of thy husband
Did it to help thee to a better husband.

Man
His better doth not breathe upon the earth.

Woman
He lives that loves thee better than he could.

Man
Name him.

Woman
Plantagenet.

Man
Why, that was he.

Woman
The selfsame name, but one of better nature.

Man
Where is he?

Woman
Here.

> *With this, the **Man** spits at her. It arrests the moment and she drops character. The **Witches** come forward, delivering a reminder.*

Woman
Why dost thou spit at me?

Man
   (finding his own language)
You just keep pushing and pushing
I mean you—

Woman
—My character.

Man
You have no shame.

Woman
What's your next line?

Man
I can't

Woman
Why?

Man
. . . because I don't know if I'm doing this right.

Woman
You're saying it's hard to play the scene because you want to do it right
Not because it actually costs you something?

Third Witch
It has to cost you something.

Man
It's hard because of the given circumstances.
You have hurt people I love
You are disrespecting me and everyone here.

Woman
—my character is . . .

Man
Your character is.
and a huge part of the scene
is that Richard is stronger than her
stronger than me.

Woman
Stronger in what sense?

Man
He is stronger in terms of his ability to coerce.
His physical power.

Woman
—because he's a man?

Man
Yes.
and stronger in will maybe?

Woman
Who says?

Man
Richard spends the entire play
Making a list of enemies
—most of whom you are related to, your own flesh and blood

and successfully killing them off.
And as Lady Anne, I just feel a little . . .

Witches and Woman
—powerless?

Man
    (*correcting*)
I'm under real threat.

Woman
And so you can't play the scene . . . why?
    Beat.
You don't find me threatening?

Man
Not really.

Woman
Not really?
Or no.

Man
. . .

Woman
Why?

Man
Because we know each other.

Woman
What if we didn't.

Man
I don't understand.

Woman
If you didn't know me
or any of them
and you came across us in the world
bumped into us
had to talk to us
Had to deal with us
—would you be threatened?

Man
If you're trying to provoke me
or get me to admit something gross
I'm not going to do it
If you want me to say that I'm inherently afraid of you
because . . .
No.
Did I come from a place
where there were more people like me
then there are people like you?
Yes.
Did I have to learn how to . . .
Am I still learning how to be—

Woman
If instead of just answering my question
You're going to give me another liberal soup speech
I'd rather you just save it.

Man
  (*to Shakespeare*)
Out of my sight! Thou dost infect mine eyes.

Woman
Thine eyes, sweet lady, have infected mine.

Man
Would they were basilisks, to strike thee dead!

Woman
I would they were, that I might die at once;
For now they kill me with a living death.
Teach not thy lip such scorn, for it was made
For kissing, lady, not for such contempt.
If thy revengeful heart cannot forgive,
Lo, here I lend thee this sharp-pointed sword,
Which if thou please to hide in this true breast,
And let the soul forth that adoreth thee,
I lay it naked to the deadly stroke,
And humbly beg the death upon my knee.

She kneels and offers her chest to his blade.

Man
I would I knew thy heart.

Woman
'Tis figured in my tongue.

Man
I fear me both are false.

Woman
Then never was man true.

*The **Woman** places a ring on his hand.*

Woman
Vouchsafe to wear this ring.

Man
Marriage?
We have to do this now?

Woman
Now.

Man
My god this is relentless.

Lady Anne's final line is interrupted by a kiss. It is a final kiss here between the two. A flipped mirror of their first encounter. Aggressive, perhaps unwanted.

Man
Wait
No you can't win that way
I want to try again.

First Witch
Are you sure?

> *A small moment here as the* **Man** *studies* **First Witch**. *She lets him. They seem to both be figuring something out as they have spent much time across the plays at odds.*

Man
Can I see your . . .
This.
Your costume.
May I?

First Witch
Sure.

Man
Can you help me put this on?
—sorry.

First Witch
Try not to apologize.
Think of that as a first step.

> *The* **First Witch** *undoes her corset and gives it him. He tries it on, but is unable to get it on alone. All three* **Witches** *carefully help him into it. We take our time to build this image.*

First Witch
What do you feel?

Man
Relief, oddly.
And I am . . .

First Witch
You are Queen Elizabeth.
    (*a breath*)
Your husband the king is dying

Man
    (*falling to Shakespeare*)
If he were dead, what will betide on me?

Second Witch
—and then . . .

First Witch
Your husband the king is dead.

Man
    (*falling closer to Queen Elizabeth*)
The loss of such a lord includes all harms.

First Witch
Lady Anne is crownèd Richard's royal queen

Third Witch
Killed and then Richard makes your children his prey.

Man
Ah, cut my lace asunder
That my pent heart may have some scope to beat,
Or else I swoon with this dead-killing news!
Pity, you ancient stones, those tender babes
Whom envy hath immured within your walls—
Rough cradle for such little pretty ones.

IV. Richard III   273

First Witch
—and as you have a daughter
Richard is coming to demand her hand in marriage.

Second Witch
Good luck.

Third Witch
. . . Last try . . .

First Witch
—and

All Witches
God save the Queen.

> *The* **Witches** *withdraw to let him play the scene. This is the final woman Richard will face off with, this evening at least. In this last attempt there is a radical shift in the* **Man**'s *approach.*
>
> *Perhaps he pulls them into an Heritage scene with all English respectability. Or perhaps his embodiment of felinity has deepened.*

Woman
   (*to the* **Man**)
Madam I would have a word with you.

Man
I have no more sons of the royal blood
For thee to slaughter.

Woman
You have a daughter.
Virtuous and fair, royal and gracious.

Man
And must she die for this? O, let her live,

And I'll corrupt her manners, stain her beauty,
Slander myself as false to Edward's bed,
Throw over her the veil of infamy.
So she may live unscarred of bleeding slaughter,
I will confess she was not Edward's daughter.

Woman
Wrong not her birth. She is a royal princess.

Man
To save her life, I'll say she is not so.

Woman
Her life is safest only in her birth.

Man
And only in that safety died her brothers.

Woman
Lo, at their birth good stars were opposite.

Man
No, to their lives ill friends were contrary.

Woman
All unavoided is the doom of destiny.

Man
True, when avoided grace makes destiny.
My babes were destined to a fairer death.

Woman
You speak as if that I had slain my cousins.

Man
Cousins, indeed, and by their uncle cozened
Of comfort, kingdom, kindred, freedom, life.
Whose hand soever launched their tender hearts,
Thy head, all indirectly, gave direction.

No doubt the murd'rous knife was dull and blunt
Till it was whetted on thy stone-hard heart,
To revel in the entrails of my lambs.

Woman
Madam, so thrive I in my enterprise
And dangerous success of bloody wars
As I intend more good to you and yours
Than ever you or yours by me were harmed!

Man
Be brief, lest that the process of thy kindness
Last longer telling than thy kindness' date.

Woman
Then know that from my soul I love thy daughter.
And do intend to make her Queen of England.

Man
Well then, who dost thou mean shall be her king?

Woman
Even he that makes her queen. Who else should be?

Man
What, thou
How canst thou woo her?

Woman
That would I learn of you,
As one being best acquainted with her humor.

Man
And wilt thou learn of me?

Woman
Madam, with all my heart.

Man
There is no other way,
Unless thou couldst put on some other shape
And not be Richard, that hath done all this.

Woman
Look what is done cannot be now amended.
Men shall deal unadvisedly sometimes,
Which after-hours gives leisure to repent.
If I did take the kingdom from your sons,
To make amends I'll give it to your daughter.
If I have killed the issue of your womb,
To quicken your increase I will beget
Mine issue of your blood upon your daughter.
A grandam's name is little less in love
Than is the doting title of a mother.

Man
What were I best to say? Her father's brother
Would be her lord? Or shall I say her uncle?
Or he that slew her brothers and her uncles?
Under what title shall I woo for thee,
That God, the law, my honor, and her love
Can make seem pleasing to her tender years?

Woman
Say I will love her everlastingly.

Man
But how long shall that title "ever" last?

Woman
Sweetly in force unto her fair life's end.

Man
But how long fairly shall her sweet life last?

Woman
As long as heaven and nature lengthens it.

Man
As long as hell and Richard likes of it.

Woman
Be eloquent in my behalf to her.

Man
An honest tale speeds best being plainly told.

Woman
Then plainly to her tell my loving tale.

Man
Plain and not honest is too harsh a style.

Woman
Your reasons are too shallow and too quick.

Man
O no, my reasons are too deep and dead—
Too deep and dead, poor infants, in their graves.

Woman
　　(*attempting to sing*)
I KNOW YOU, YOU
AND YOU KNOW ME
I KNOW—

Man
Stop.

Woman
I swear by . . .

Man
—by nothing, for this is no oath.
Swear then by something that thou hast
not wronged.

Woman
Then, by myself—

Man
Thyself is self-misused.

Woman
Now, by the world—

Man
'Tis full of thy foul wrongs.
What canst thou swear by now?

Woman
If, with dear heart's love,
I tender not thy beauteous princely daughter.
In her consists my happiness and thine.
Without her follows to myself and thee,
Herself, the land, and many a Christian soul,
Death, desolation, ruin, and decay.
It cannot be avoided but by this;
It will not be avoided but by this.
Therefore, dear mother—I must call you so—
Be the attorney of my love to her;
Urge the necessity and state of times,
And be not peevish found in great designs.

> *With this the* **Woman** *as Richard wins. A moment of physical exploration begins here which will punctuate at the end of the scene. Either woman begins tightening* **Man**'s *corset to the limit or taking it off, or pulling him inescapably closer with each string.*

IV. Richard III   279

Man
Shall I forget myself to be myself?

Woman
Ay, if your self's remembrance wrong yourself.

Man
Yet thou didst kill my children.

Woman
But in your daughter's womb I bury them.

Man
I go. Write to me very shortly,
And you shall understand from me her mind.

Woman
Bear her my true love's kiss; and so, farewell.

> *An attempt at a kiss. This could lead to failure, or it could lead to a goodbye. After this moment, the* **Man** *takes off his corset and hands it back to the* **First Witch**. *He retreats to the* **Band**, *and while taking a break of sorts stays vigilant of the* **Woman** *and Witches.*
>
> *The* **Witches** *try their best to keep their distance from the* **Woman**.

Woman
Was ever woman in this humor wooed?
Was ever woman in this humor won?

Third Witch
What do you mean?
Was there ever a woman this Manipulated?
Led on?
Lied to?
Promised something and given nothing?
Kissed and killed?

There were many
There are many
> *Beat.*

I can't take this anymore.

Second Witch
We have to just get to the end of the story.

Second Witch
Believe me
The end will come.

Song 7: We the People

Second Witch
ALL SOMEONE HAS TO DO
IS FILL IN THE SPOTS
THE ONES THAT KEEP US APART
AND DANCE BETWEEN THE EARS

ALL SOMEONE HAS TO DO
IS SPEAK TO THE WORLD
ITS WORST PARTS
THAT KEEP ROLLIN ON.

Witches and Man
KEEP ON ROLLIN ON.

First Witch
I KNOW YOU'RE SICK
BECAUSE I AM TOO

Woman
I GOT SHIVERS AND CHILLS
I WANT EVERYTHING ALL THE TIME
TOO MUCH WINE
TOO MANY PILLS
TOO MUCH LOOKING DOWN

First Witch
WE THE PEOPLE GOT A FLU
THE KIND THAT STICKS AROUND

BECAUSE
NO MATTER THE PLACE
PEOPLE FALL IN LINE
NO MATTER THE TIME,
THEY ALWAYS FALL IN LINE
THEY KNOW IT'S ALL WRONG
STILL PEOPLE FALL IN LINE
BEST WAY TO STAY ALIVE

All
NO MATTER THE PLACE
PEOPLE FALL IN LINE
NO MATTER THE TIME,
THEY ALWAYS FALL IN LINE
THEY KNOW IT'S ALL WRONG
STILL PEOPLE FALL IN LINE
BEST WAY TO STAY ALIVE

First Witch
I'M NO BETTER

Second Witch
I'M NO BETTER

Third Witch
I'M NO BETTER

Second Witch
I COULD BE BETTER

First Witch
BUT I'M NO BETTER
IF MY NECK'S ON THE LINE
... I RESPOND IN TIME
OH!

First Witch
I'M NO BETTER

Second Witch
I'M NO BETTER

Third Witch
I'M NO BETTER

Second Witch
I COULD BE BETTER

First Witch
BUT I'M NO BETTER
IF MY NECK'S ON THE LINE
. . . I RESPOND IN TIME

First Witch
NO MATTER THE PLACE
PEOPLE FALL IN LINE
NO MATTER THE TIME, THEY ALWAYS FALL IN LINE
THEY KNOW IT'S ALL WRONG
STILL PEOPLE FALL IN LINE
IT'S JUST THE EASIEST WAY TO STAY ALIVE

First Witch
Listen.
We don't need to go through all of this play
to know what happens.
War?
We live with it.
Violence?
We got it.

Woman
But you liked it
You laughed at me
—you all did

(to audience)
You enjoyed the villain.
You enjoyed Richard.

First Witch
*(to **Woman** and audience)*
If, when you see these plays
you laugh a little too long at the bad parts
If Iago is starting to make sense
Maybe we need to let it rest.
Maybe we need a new story.

Woman
People kept telling me that
"Rewrite the ending"
But I couldn't.

Man
(from afar)
Maybe a new ending will make sense for someone else.

> *The **Woman** looks around at the ensemble, she grows concerned. It's clear they are ready for a new way, one perhaps even she cannot imagine.*

Woman
What would a new story even be?

First Witch
Once upon a time there was a girl . . .

Woman
No.

Second Witch
Once upon a time there was a WOMAN . . .

Woman
No

Third Witch
Once upon a time there was a wife

Woman
No.
> *Beat.*

It's hard isn't it?
Maybe it could go . . .

Third Witch
One day,

First Witch
Maybe it could go . . .

Second Witch
we hope

Man
One day maybe.

Third Witch
One day.

Man and Witches
we pray.

First Witch
And if that day isn't *today*
then you should just do one last thing right and be done.
Don't play their way.
Don't get payback.
Just be on your way.
Either up your street, to find a new way
or to your grave
but do *one* thing right.

Woman

I guess the one thing
I wanted to do
—I should of done
I guess I should say that
The one person all of this was for
—that all these plays were for
Was her.
For me, her name was Rachel.
This person was my *family*.
and she should be here.
    (*to the* **Witches** *and audience*)
I'm sure you have a Rachel.
I'm sure you if you try and think about this person
you can see her face.
and when you wind the clock back
you can see the corners and lines of where
they were headed
but it doesn't make anything easier.
It doesn't make it make sense.
So I started looking at these plays
because I saw the lines between these *very*
stories
and her.

And I became *a n g r y*.

Witches and Man

I know. / I hear you

Woman
    (*leaving Richard behind*)
And I was angry
Because I wondered
why things can't change more?
I am not angry because a white man wrote some plays.
I'm angry because they are still relevant
and that's our fault.
and with Richard III

It feels so inevitable that the women in the play
will suffer.
And that's how I feel for her
For Rachel.

   Beat.

But there was a song I wrote
For her.
I meant to sing it earlier
But it got lost somewhere
in all these stories.

   Beat.

It goes like this.

<u>Song 8: Queen</u>

DARLING WHEN I'M QUEEN
I'LL GET JUST WHAT I NEED
THEY'LL GET DOWN ON THEIR KNEES
YOU'LL SEE!

DARLING WHEN I'M QUEEN
IM GONNA BURN DOWN EVERYTHING
I'LL GET JUST WHAT I NEED
YOU'LL SEE!

WHEN I'M QUEEN
HIGH UP HOLY HOLY
HOW LOW HOW LOW
HOW LOW
HOW FAR MUST I GO!

SO TAKE ME SOMEWHERE LOW
WHERE THE LIGHTS
WON'T EVEN GO
LET ME GO ALONE
TO MY LOVE

WHEN I'M QUEEN
WAY UP HOLY

IV. Richard III

HOW FAR HOW FAR
HOW FAR CAN I GO . . .

> *After this song the ensemble leads her to a new and fourth microphone that has been revealed, closer to where the **Witches** normally live. It is her final resting place for this show. Perhaps, she resists.*

Man
It's okay.
Let it rest.

Woman
How?

Man
We did pretty well.
And if you took us around all over again
I'd do it again.
every man
every woman
Every character.
Until we figured it out.
Because I want to figure it out.
   (bad but essential idea)
But I think
for now
someone else has to try.
and that's okay.

> *With his help she joins them, leaving her center microphone vacant.*

All
HALLELUJAH
HALLELUJAH
HALLELUJAH
HALLE!

HALLELUJAH
HALLELUJAH
HALLELUJAH
HALLE!

HALLELUJAH
HALLELUJAH
HALLELUJAH
HALLELUJAH

First Witch
(*audience*)
We're talking to you
All of you.
Or will it be just one of you?
Is there anyone out there who needs to speak a name?

> *Here, if any ensemble or band members with they can speak the names of their loved ones. Their friends. Their women. Their othered people for whom this work is for.*

First Witch
What's their story?
What's *your* story?

All
HALLELUJAH
HALLELUJAH
HALLELUJAH
HALLE!

HALLELUJAH
HALLELUJAH
HALLELUJAH
HALLE!

HALLELUJAH
HALLELUJAH

HALLELUJAH
HALLELUJAH

> *Will someone take the mic? Are there cries of names coming from the audience? Lights fall as the ensemble and band's voices shake the walls.*

END.

Discover. Read. Listen. Watch.

A NEW WAY TO ENGAGE WITH PLAYS

This award-winning digital library features over 3,000 playtexts, 400 audio plays, 300 hours of video and 360 scholarly books.

Playtexts published by Methuen Drama, The Arden Shakespeare, Faber & Faber, Playwrights Canada Press, Aurora Metro Books and Nick Hern Books.

Audio Plays from L.A. Theatre Works featuring classic and modern works from the oeuvres of leading American playwrights.

Video collections including films of live performances from the RSC, The Globe and The National Theatre, as well as acting masterclasses and BBC feature films and documentaries.

FIND OUT MORE:
www.dramaonlinelibrary.com • @dramaonlinelib

Methuen Drama Modern Plays

include

Bola Agbaje
Edward Albee
Ayad Akhtar
Jean Anouilh
John Arden
Peter Barnes
Sebastian Barry
Clare Barron
Alistair Beaton
Brendan Behan
Edward Bond
William Boyd
Bertolt Brecht
Howard Brenton
Amelia Bullmore
Anthony Burgess
Leo Butler
Jim Cartwright
Lolita Chakrabarti
Caryl Churchill
Lucinda Coxon
Tim Crouch
Shelagh Delaney
Ishy Din
Claire Dowie
David Edgar
David Eldridge
Dario Fo
Michael Frayn
John Godber
James Graham
David Greig
John Guare
Lauren Gunderson
Peter Handke
David Harrower
Jonathan Harvey
Robert Holman
David Ireland
Sarah Kane

Barrie Keeffe
Jasmine Lee-Jones
Anders Lustgarten
Duncan Macmillan
David Mamet
Patrick Marber
Martin McDonagh
Arthur Miller
Alistair McDowall
Tom Murphy
Phyllis Nagy
Anthony Neilson
Peter Nichols
Ben Okri
Joe Orton
Vinay Patel
Joe Penhall
Luigi Pirandello
Stephen Poliakoff
Lucy Prebble
Peter Quilter
Mark Ravenhill
Philip Ridley
Willy Russell
Jackie Sibblies Drury
Sam Shepard
Martin Sherman
Chris Shinn
Wole Soyinka
Simon Stephens
Kae Tempest
Anne Washburn
Laura Wade
Theatre Workshop
Timberlake Wertenbaker
Roy Williams
Snoo Wilson
Frances Ya-Chu Cowhig
Benjamin Zephaniah

Methuen Drama Contemporary Dramatists

include

John Arden (two volumes)
Arden & D'Arcy
Peter Barnes (three volumes)
Sebastian Barry
Mike Bartlett
Clare Barron
Brad Birch
Dermot Bolger
Edward Bond (ten volumes)
Howard Brenton (two volumes)
Leo Butler (two volumes)
Richard Cameron
Jim Cartwright
Caryl Churchill (two volumes)
Complicite
Sarah Daniels (two volumes)
Nick Darke
David Edgar (three volumes)
David Eldridge (two volumes)
Ben Elton
Per Olov Enquist
Dario Fo (two volumes)
Michael Frayn (four volumes)
John Godber (four volumes)
Paul Godfrey
James Graham (two volumes)
David Greig
John Guare
Lee Hall (two volumes)
Katori Hall
Peter Handke
Jonathan Harvey (two volumes)
Iain Heggie
Israel Horovitz
Declan Hughes
Terry Johnson (three volumes)
Sarah Kane
Barrie Keeffe
Bernard-Marie Koltès (two volumes)
Franz Xaver Kroetz
Kwame Kwei-Armah
David Lan
Bryony Lavery
Deborah Levy
Doug Lucie
Alistair MacDowall
Sabrina Mahfouz
David Mamet (six volumes)
Patrick Marber
Martin McDonagh
Duncan McLean
David Mercer (two volumes)
Anthony Minghella (two volumes)
Rory Mullarkey
Tom Murphy (six volumes)
Phyllis Nagy
Anthony Neilson (three volumes)
Peter Nichol (two volumes)
Philip Osment
Gary Owen
Louise Page
Stewart Parker (two volumes)
Joe Penhall (two volumes)
Stephen Poliakoff (three volumes)
David Rabe (two volumes)
Mark Ravenhill (three volumes)
Christina Reid
Philip Ridley (two volumes)
Willy Russell
Eric-Emmanuel Schmitt
Ntozake Shange
Sam Shepard (two volumes)
Martin Sherman (two volumes)
Christopher Shinn (two volumes)
Joshua Sobel
Wole Soyinka (five volumes)
Simon Stephens (five volumes)
Shelagh Stephenson
David Storey (three volumes)
C. P. Taylor
Sue Townsend
Judy Upton (two volumes)
Michel Vinaver (two volumes)
Arnold Wesker (two volumes)
Peter Whelan
Michael Wilcox
Roy Williams (four volumes)
David Williamson
Snoo Wilson (two volumes)
David Wood (two volumes)
Victoria Wood

Methuen Drama Student Editions

Alan Ayckbourn *Confusions* • **Mike Bartlett** *Earthquakes in London* • **Aphra Behn** *The Rover* • **Alice Birch** *Revolt. She Said. Revolt Again* • **Edward Bond** *Lear* • *Saved* • **Bertolt Brecht** *The Caucasian Chalk Circle* • *Fear and Misery in the Third Reich* • *The Good Person of Szechwan* • *Life of Galileo* • *Mother Courage and her Children* • *The Resistible Rise of Arturo Ui* • *The Threepenny Opera* • **Jon Brittain** *Rotterdam* • **Georg Büchner** *Woyzeck* • **Anton Chekhov** *The Cherry Orchard* • *The Seagull* • *Three Sisters* • *Uncle Vanya* • **Caryl Churchill** *Serious Money* • *Top Girls* • **Shelagh Delaney** *A Taste of Honey* • **Inua Ellams** *Barber Shop Chronicles* • **Euripides** *Elektra* • *Medea* • **Dario Fo** *Accidental Death of an Anarchist* • **Michael Frayn** *Copenhagen* • **John Galsworthy** *Strife* • **Nikolai Gogol** *The Government Inspector* • **Carlo Goldoni** *A Servant to Two Masters* • **James Graham** *This House* • **Tanika Gupta** *The Empress* • **Katori Hall** *The Mountaintop* • **Lorraine Hansberry** *A Raisin in the Sun* • **Robert Holman** *Across Oka* • **Henrik Ibsen** *A Doll's House* • *Ghosts* • *Hedda Gabler* • **Sarah Kane** *4.48 Psychosis* • *Blasted* • **Charlotte Keatley** *My Mother Said I Never Should* • **Dennis Kelly** *DNA* • **Bernard Kops** *Dreams of Anne Frank* • **Federico García Lorca** *Blood Wedding* • *Doña Rosita the Spinster* (bilingual edition) • *The House of Bernarda Alba* (bilingual edition) • *Yerma* (bilingual edition) • **David Mamet** *Glengarry Glen Ross* • *Oleanna* • **Patrick Marber** *Closer* • **John Marston** *The Malcontent* • **Martin McDonagh** *The Lieutenant of Inishmore* • *The Lonesome West* • *The Beauty Queen of Leenane* • *The Cripple of Inishmaan* • **Alistair McDowall** *Pomona* • **John McGrath** *The Cheviot, the Stag and the Black, Black Oil* • **Arthur Miller** *All My Sons* • *The Crucible* • *A View from the Bridge* • *Death of a Salesman* • *The Price* • *After the Fall* • *The Last Yankee* • *A Memory of Two Mondays* • *Broken Glass* • *Incident at Vichy* • *The American Clock* • *The Ride Down Mt. Morgan* • **Joe Orton** *Loot* • **Joe Penhall** *Blue/Orange* • **Luigi Pirandello** *Six Characters in Search of an Author* • **Lucy Prebble** *Enron* • **Mark Ravenhill** *Shopping and F***ing* • **Reginald Rose** *Twelve Angry Men* • **Willy Russell** *Blood Brothers* • *Educating Rita* • **Lemn Sissay** Benjamin Zephaniah's *Refugee Boy* • **Sophocles** *Antigone* • *Oedipus the King* • **Wole Soyinka** *Death and the King's Horseman* • **Simon Stephens** *Punk Rock* • *Pornography* • **Shelagh Stephenson** *The Memory of Water* • **August Strindberg** *Miss Julie* • **J. M. Synge** *The Playboy of the Western World* • **Kae Tempest** *Wasted* • **Theatre Workshop** *Oh What a Lovely War* • **Laura Wade** *Posh* • **Frank Wedekind** *Spring Awakening* • **Timberlake Wertenbaker** *Our Country's Good* • **Arnold Wesker** *The Merchant* • **Peter Whelan** *The Accrington Pals* • **Oscar Wilde** *The Importance of Being Earnest* • **Roy Williams** *Sing Yer Heart Out for the Lads* • **Tennessee Williams** *A Streetcar Named Desire* • *The Glass Menagerie* • *Cat on a Hot Tin Roof* • *Sweet Bird of Youth*

Methuen Drama World Classics
include

Jean Anouilh (two volumes)
John Arden (two volumes)
Brendan Behan
Aphra Behn
Bertolt Brecht (eight volumes)
Georg Büchner
Mikhail Bulgakov
Pedro Calderón
Karel Čapek
Peter Nichols (two volumes)
Anton Chekhov
Noël Coward (nine volumes)
Georges Feydeau (two volumes)
Eduardo De Filippo
Max Frisch (two volumes)
John Galsworthy
Nikolai Gogol (two volumes)
Maxim Gorky (two volumes)
Harley Granville Barker
(two volumes)
Victor Hugo
Henrik Ibsen (six volumes)
Alfred Jarry
Federico García Lorca
(three volumes)
Pierre Marivaux
Mustapha Matura
David Mercer
(two volumes)
Arthur Miller (six volumes)
Molière
Pierre de Musset
Joe Orton
A. W. Pinero
Luigi Pirandello
Terence Rattigan
W. Somerset Maugham
August Strindberg
(three volumes)
J. M. Synge
Ramón del Valle-Inclán
Frank Wedekind
Oscar Wilde
Tennessee Williams

Methuen Drama
Classical Greek Dramatists

Aeschylus Plays: One
(Persians, Seven Against Thebes, Suppliants,
Prometheus Bound)

Aeschylus Plays: Two
(Oresteia: Agamemnon, Libation-Bearers, Eumenides)

Aristophanes Plays: One
(Acharnians, Knights, Peace, Lysistrata)

Aristophanes Plays: Two
(Wasps, Clouds, Birds, Festival Time, Frogs)

Aristophanes & Menander: New Comedy
(Women in Power, Wealth, The Malcontent,
The Woman from Samos)

Euripides Plays: One
(Medea, The Phoenician Women, Bacchae)

Euripides Plays: Two
(Hecuba, The Women of Troy, Iphigeneia at Aulis, Cyclops)

Euripides Plays: Three
(Alkestis, Helen, Ion)

Euripides Plays: Four
(Elektra, Orestes, Iphigeneia in Tauris)

Euripides Plays: Five
(Andromache, Herakles' Children, Herakles)

Euripides Plays: Six
(Hippolytos, Suppliants, Rhesos)

Sophocles Plays: One
(Oedipus the King, Oedipus at Colonus, Antigone)

Sophocles Plays: Two
(Ajax, Women of Trachis, Electra, Philoctetes)

For a complete listing of
Methuen Drama titles, visit:
www.bloomsbury.com/drama

Follow us on Twitter and keep up to date
with our news and publications
@MethuenDrama